Greece & Rome

NEW SURVEYS IN THE CLASSICS No. 14

EURIPIDES

BY C. COLLARD

Published for the Classical Association

OXFORD: AT THE CLARENDON PRESS

1981

Oxford University Press, Walton Street, Oxford OX2 6DP
London Glasgow New York Toronto
Delhi Bombay Calcutta Madras Karachi
Kuala Lumpur Singapore Hong Kong Tokyo
Nairobi Dar Es Salaam Cape Town
Melbourne Auckland

and associate companies in
Beirut Berlin Ibadan Mexico City

ISBN 0 903035 11 1

Printed in Great Britain
at the University Press, Oxford
by Eric Buckley
Printer to the University

INTRODUCTORY NOTE

I concentrate on the surviving complete plays; and I have tried to write my main text for Euripides' wider student public, sixth-formers and especially undergraduates, many of them without Greek, and for some at least of their teachers. In the notes and bibliographical appendix (on which abbreviated references in the notes depend) I aim more widely, but cite only the most helpful, important, and recent literature, where possible in English. This Survey is not for specialists, but the sign 'bibl.' often suggests a starting-point for deeper enquiry.

I thank Ian McAuslan for an editor's patience, and both him and Tony Brothers for criticizing parts of a draft.

C.C.

CONTENTS

I. THE EXTANT WORK

(a) *A representative sample?*

Euripides' dramatic career lasted from 455 B.C. to his death, aged 70 or so, in 406.[1] Early on, he gained official performances at the Great Dionysiac Festival about every five years, it seems; in mid-career, every two or three; at the end, almost every year – but he won first prize on only 4 out of 22 occasions, the first in 441, the last, posthumously, in 406 (for the known details, see the 'Table' below).[2] Twenty-two performances give a total of 66 tragedies, and that many were indeed known in text or at least title (together with some spurious works) to the Alexandrian scholars who edited Euripides in the third century B.C.[3] Antiquity itself, however, lacked sure information about the corresponding 22 satyric or pro-satyric dramas, let alone their texts; and we know only 8 or 9 titles.[4]

From this *oeuvre* some 16 tragedies survive complete, but all from the second part of the career, the earliest *Medea* of 431; and we have *Alcestis*, substituted for the satyr-play in the production of 438 but largely tragic in manner; and the late, purely satyric *Cyclops*. In our dependence on later plays for assessing Euripides in the round, we seem to be as disadvantaged as for Aeschylus (7 tragedies out of some 70, and from the last third of his career) and for Sophocles (7 out of some 90, and from the latter two-thirds). The sheer number of complete plays is much greater, however, and for the lost ones we have many more sizeable fragments, on papyrus or in quotation by other authors (though again mostly from later plays);[5] a steady accretion of smaller papyrus fragments;[6] richer and more various secondary written evidence, mainly literary echoes, parody, comments, résumés, and even translations;[7] and more apparent reflections of play-scenes in vase-paintings.[8] This greater richness is due to Euripides' wider popularity and more lasting influence from the century after his death, in Hellenistic and Greco-Roman times, whether upon later drama or in re-performance, reading, or education, especially rhetorical.[9]

Despite this abundance, appreciation of Euripides must still rest largely on the complete plays. Their shapes, features, and habits are visible fact; they help reconstruct the lost plays and locate them in Euripides' career, while the hypothetical and often disputed content of those serves rather to illustrate and amplify our appreciation – often, it is true, suggestively.

Likely historical sequence of the extant and some fragmentary plays[10]
(the 'bracketing' in play-titles indicates abbreviations used later)

Date	Extant	Fragmentary	Evidence for date (* = inferential)
455		Peliades	'Life', ed. Schwartz, p. 4.2 (first production)
441		(first victory)	Marmor Parium 60
438	Alc(estis) (pro-satyric)	Cretan Women, Alcmaeon in Psophis, Telephus	Hypothesis, Alc. (2nd prize)
431	Med(ea)	Philoctetes, Diktys, Theristai (sat.)	Hypothesis, Med. (3rd prize)
430–428	H(era)cl(i)d(ae)		*, metrical: Webster (1967), p. 101; Lesky (1972), p. 348
428	Hipp(olytus) (revised from earlier production)		Hypothesis, Hipp. (1st prize)
?425	And(romache)		*, metrical: ed. Stevens, pp. 15–19
before 423	Hec(uba)		allusions in Ar. Clouds (423); metrical
423		Cresphontes	*, parody, Ar. frag. 109 Kock: ed. Musso, p. xxvii f.
?423	Supp(lices)		*, metrical: ed. Collard, pp. 8–14
422		Erechtheus	Plut., Vit.Nic. 9.5
after 420		Phaethon	*, metrical: ed. Diggle, pp. 47–9; after 415, Webster (1967), p. 220 n. 68
?before 415	H(ercules) F(urens)		*, but (metrical) after 415, Webster (1967), p. 163
before 415	El(ectra)		*, metrical: Lesky (1972), pp. 392–4
415	Tro(ades)	Alexandros, Palamedes, Sisyphos (sat.)	Aelian, Var.Hist. II.8 (2nd prize)
before 412	I(phigenia in) T(auris)		*, metrical: Lesky (1972), p. 405
?before 412	Ion		*, metrical: Lesky (1972), p. 425
412	Hel(en)	Andromeda	schol. Ar. Thes. 1012, 1040, Frogs 53
?412	Cyclops (sat.)		*, see n. 4
411–408, ?409	Pho(enissae)	Antiope, Hypsipyle	schol. Ar. Frogs 53: see Webster (1967), p. 163, Lesky (1972), p. 444; Antiope ?408–7, ed. Kambitsis, pp. xxxi–iv
408	Or(estes)		schol. Or. 371
after 406	I(phigenia in) A(ulis), Bacc(hae)	Alcmaeon in Corinth	all 3 posthumous: schol. Ar. Frogs 67 (1st prize)

(b) *Text: transmission and quality*

The medieval manuscript tradition is in two main parts.[11] In one, nine plays, *Hec., Or., Pho., And., Med., Hipp., Alc., Tro.* (the order varies) – and the spurious *Rhesus*[12] – together with commentators' scholia, appear to stem from a selective, annotated edition made in later antiquity and based perhaps on a centuries-long contraction of the popular or widely read plays into a small corpus (analogous editions are posited for Aeschylus and Sophocles). The other part, which lacks scholia, carries not only these nine plays in a slightly variant tradition, but a further ten: *Bacc.* (which seems nevertheless to have belonged originally to the 'selection'), and the so-called 'alphabetic' plays *Hel., El., HF, Hcld., Ion, Supp., IA, IT, Cyc.* (: Greek initial letters E, H, I, K). These must be partial and wholly accidental survivors from a very old, perhaps papyrus, complete edition of Euripides in which the plays were ordered alphabetically.

The 'select' tradition is 'open', its medieval manuscripts irreducible to a convincing family-tree. About ten 'older' MSS (*C.* 11–14 A.D.), of differing compass, are important, but their relationship varies from play to play; so also does it between that group and the even more confused mass of 'recent' or 'later' MSS (*C.* 13–15 A.D.) of the three plays much re-edited by late Byzantine scholars, *Hec., Or., Pho.* (again, compare similar 'triads' of Aeschylus and Sophocles). The 'alphabetic' tradition has only two, very closely related MSS (early *C.* 14) – indeed, one of these has only rare independent value.

For about half the extant plays, then, the main tradition is comparatively rich; and it is supplemented by ancient scholia, by ancient writers or later anthologists quoting these plays – but also by fragmentary papyrus texts of Euripides from the period *C.* 4 B.C. to *C.* 6 A.D. The 'alphabetic' plays in contrast depend on what is almost a *codex unicus*, while secondary evidence from papyrus or quotations is much thinner.[13] Neither tradition, primary or secondary, permits reconstruction of the text before the Alexandrian edition of the *C.* 3 B.C. (except in a very few places where older papyri survive), by which time it had already been impaired and sometimes obviously interpolated.[14]

Euripides' text in the best modern editions nonetheless looks surprisingly good; editors' total despair in the face of physical damage is infrequent; and the quality is almost as high in the 'alphabetic' as in the 'select' plays. Further significant improvement must wait upon discovery of entirely new evidence, for little marked benefit to the text itself will come from elucidation of the tangled Byzantine MSS. Conjectural emendation too has long been prey to diminishing returns.[15] Gilbert Murray said 80 years ago that Euripides needs interpretation, and not emendation.[16]

4 THE EXTANT WORK

NOTES

1. 'Biography': best review of evidence, modern literature: Lesky (1972), pp. 275–80; cf. Webster (1967), pp. 12–30, esp. 20 ff.
2. For E.'s contemporary reception see R. E. Wycherley, 'Aristophanes and E.', *G & R* 15 (1946), 98–107; P. T. Stevens, 'E. and the Athenians', *JHS* 76 (1956), 87–94; V. Martin, in *Entretiens*, pp. 245–83; Rau, pp. 19–97 and bibl.; R. G. Ussher, *Aristophanes* (Oxford, 1979), pp. 17 f., 20 f.
3. Titles, productions, and dates – certain, likely, and suggested – are most helpfully presented by Webster (1967), pp. 1–9, 31–2, 116–17, 163–5, 238, pages which rather conceal earlier scholars' immense work, esp. U. von Wilamowitz, *Analecta Euripidea* (Berlin, 1875), pp. 131–93; T. Zielinski, *Tragodumenon* (Cracow, 1925), pp. 134–240 (on his metrical criteria of date see T. B. L. Webster, *WS* 79 (1966), 112–20 and Dale, ed. *Helen*, pp. xxiv–viii); E. B. Ceadel, *CQ* 35 (1941), 66–89; cf. M. Fernandez Galiano, 'Estado actual de los problemas de cronologia euripidea', *EClas* 11 (1967), 321–54.
4. For E.'s satyr-plays see Conacher, pp. 317–26; Lesky (1972), pp. 499–504; Ussher ed. *Cyclops*, pp. 171–93, (bibl.) 221–7. I do not discuss *Cyclops*, dated to 412 B.C. by Ussher, pp. 193–204.
5. Larger pieces: *Alexandros* (415 B.C.), *Antiope* (c. 410), *Erechtheus* (422), *Hypsipyle* (c. 410), *Phaethon* (after 420) – but also *Telephus* (438).
6. All papyri: R. Pack, *The Greek and Latin Literary Texts from Greco-Roman Egypt* (Ann Arbor, 1965²); F. Stoessl, *RE* Suppl.-Bd.XI (1968), 658–70; B. E. Donovan, *Euripides-Papyri I: Texts from Oxyrhynchus* (Toronto, 1969); T. B. L. Webster, *Greek Tragedy* (Oxford, 1971), pp. 28–30; cf. my Appendix (iii).
7. Evaluated by Webster (1967), pp. 9 ff. Papyri with alphabetized Euripidean 'play-summaries' are noteworthy, esp. POxy 2455 edited, with others found by 1967, by C. Austin, *Nova Fragmenta Euripidea* (Berlin, 1968), pp. 88–103; cf. Zuntz (1963), pp. 129–46.
8. L. Séchan, *Etudes sur la tragédie grecque dans ses rapports avec la céramique* (Paris, 1926); Webster (1967), pp. 10 f., (lost plays) 297–307 and *Monuments illustrating Tragedy and Satyr-play*, 2nd. ed., *BICS* Suppl. 20 (1967) (3rd. ed. promised by J. R. Green); A. D. Trendall, T. B. L. Webster, *Illustrations of Greek Drama* (London, 1971).
9. '*Nachleben*': for a basic bibliography see the Appendix (viii).
10. Similar but fuller 'Tables' in Webster (1967), pp. 3–5 and Stoessl (n. 6 above).
11. This section is necessarily merest outline. For the whole, complex picture, and a good review of work on its problems, see Lesky (1972), pp. 280–86 (his (1967) treatment, pp. 209–12 is outdated) and, since then, esp. K. Matthiessen, *Studien zur Textüberlieferung der Hekabe des E.* (Heidelberg, 1974) (bibl.). The best things in English are Barrett, ed. *Hippolytos*, pp. 45–90 and Zuntz (1965), esp. pp. 249–88.
12. Suspect in antiquity itself, but still thought by some to be genuine and an early work, esp. W. Ritchie, *The Authenticity of the Rhesus of E.* (Cambridge, 1964) (bibl.). Most likely it is a *C.* 4 B.C. confection, passed off as E.'s play: E. Fraenkel, *Gnomon* 37 (1965), 228–41; Webster (1968), p. 122; H. D. F. Kitto, 'The *Rhesus* and related matters', *YCS* 25 (1977), 317–50.
13. Such papyri therefore have special interest and value: on e.g. the now famous POxy 2336 (*Hel.* 630–74) see esp. Zuntz (1965), pp. 217–48 and D. C. C. Young, *GRBS* 15 (1974), 39–56, and for PHib II.179 (*HF* 137–43, 146–60) see R. Kannicht, *ZPE* 21 (1976), 117–33.
14. Interpolation is worst in *Pho.* and *IA*. D. L. Page, *Actors' Interpolations in Greek Tragedy* (Oxford, 1934) (esp. on *IA*) and M. D. Reeve, 'Interpolation in Greek Tragedy', I, *GRBS* 13 (1972), 247–65; II, 451–74; III, 14 (1973), 145–71 (bibl.) take suspicion often too far. For *Pho.* see esp. E. Fraenkel, *Zu den Phoinissen des E.* (München, 1963); Reeve, II; M. W. Haslam, *GRBS* 16 (1975), 149–74 and *CQ* 26 (1976), 4–10; D. J. Mastronarde, *Phoenix* 32 (1978), 105–28 (important methodologically). For possible major loss in *Hcld.* see A. Lesky, *YCS* 25 (1977), 227–38 (bibl.); for the disputed prologues in *IA* see (corrupted) C. W. Willink, *CQ* 21 (1971), 343–64 and D. Bain, *CQ* 27 (1977), 10–26; (sound) B. M. W. Knox, *YCS* 22 (1972), 239–61.
15. The room still for conjecture is demonstrated by J. Jackson, *Marginalia Scaenica* (Oxford, 1955); J. Diggle, *PCPhS* 15 (1969), 30–59 and many subsequent papers; T. C. W. Stinton, *JHS* 97 (1977), 137–54.
16. OCT Vol. I, 1902, xi. For editions and commentaries see the Appendix (iii, v).

II. PLOTS AND PERSONS

(a) *Mainly on plots and settings*

Critics sometimes divide the plays into approximate chronological groups according to form, theme, motive, and patterns of action.[1] A single criterion may group plays quite sharply (the so-called 'tragicomic' *IT*, *Ion*, and *Hel.* of the late 410s, for example);[2] but a second may produce different groupings, or none at all, like the pervasive motif of 'deliverance' (below) or attitude to myth.[3] Some plays are 'out of period', like the very late, thematically concentrated and formally strict *Bacc.* In sum, such groupings allow too little to natural or deliberate change in technique, or to reversion to earlier style.

The *Troades* of 415 nevertheless seems to mark a major divide, probably by accident – an impression increased by its own singularity of composition among the extant plays (are its own content and form, essentially illustrative episodes on the theme of war's brutality, a function of its final place in the most connected trilogy Euripides wrote?).[4] Before *Tro.*, most plays are tragic or pathetic in tone; after it, lighter or at least ambiguous. Early plays body out major, dominating figures and their protracted agony more consistently than later; contrast Medea, Phaedra, Andromache (name-play) and Hecuba (name-play), with principal characters later: only Heracles (before 415?), Orestes (name-play), Pentheus, Agamemnon (*IA*) and perhaps Hypsipyle are shown at comparable length and intensity.[5] Also, later plays fill up with persons who compete for attention, often theatrically, and so diffuse interest. Yet the marked tendency to episodic dramaturgy (see § III(a) below) is hinted earlier: it threatens the unity of *Hcld.*, in the final scene of Alcmena and Eurystheus; of the seemingly bipartite *Hec.* (suffering and revenge); and especially of *And.* (Andromache disappears, 765); the three superficially centrifugal actions of *HF* (persecution; rescue; destruction and 'rescue') are found logically coherent in theme.[6]

The type of plot most consistently favoured by Euripides tells the survival, physical or mental, of persecution or other grim circumstance.[7] Straightforward 'suppliant dramas' tend to come early, in which groups (*Hcld.*, *Supp.*) or individuals (*And.*), in refuge at altars, are saved through disinterested intervention – but the later *HF* uses the motif strongly at its start (Heracles' family in refuge from the tyrant Lycus), just as it shapes important episodes of *Hel.* (1 ff.: Helen at the shrine of Proteus) and *Ion* (1250 ff.: Creusa's refuge at the altar).[8] In plays of this general style, at any date, survival or deliverance is seldom to happiness unalloyed (the ends of *IT*, *Ion* and *Hel.*, already mentioned as a 'group', come nearest); rather it is bitter-sweet, or ambiguous, often leaving pain for self or others which must be lived with. In *Supp.* the mothers recover their dead sons only to begin endless grief (778–92, 955–79, 1114–22). Heracles saves his family, only to fulfil Lycus' purpose when he kills them in his madness; the irony is terrible enough, but he must then fight his hero's conscience to survive himself (1146–62, esp. 1214–1310 and ff.). Apollo perfunctorily rescues Orestes at the end of *Or.* from likely death and his own crazy spite against Menelaus, and we ask, Why? Even in the light, early *Alc.*, one wonders whether Admetus deserves his wife's fairy-tale deliverance from Death.

Disaster is often avoided, and escape planned, after last-minute or fortuitous recognitions and interventions. Orestes' self-sacrifice to save his friend Pylades brings discovery by his sister Iphigenia who will otherwise kill him (*IT* 683 ff.); then the three plan escape (902 ff.). The dove which drinks by chance the poisoned cup frustrates Creusa's intent upon her unknown son Ion (*Ion* 1181–1228); then, with Ion threatening her sanctuary at the altar, recognition is achieved when the priestess comes to give Ion his birth-tokens (1320 ff.). Amphiaraus is just in time to save Hypsipyle from Eurydice, the death of whose baby son she has indirectly caused (*Hypsipyle* frag. 60. 2–36, ed. Bond).[9]

Such sudden turns both break and create tension. Further excitement, and sometimes horror, depend on planned deception, in the lighter pieces like *IT* and *Hel.* (note how both plays employ escape by ship, *IT* 999 ff., *Hel.* 1055 ff.), and in more heavily charged settings. Medea uses both Creon and Aegeus in punishing Jason, whose own better nature she exploits (*Med.* 866 ff.), so that we end by shifting our sympathy to him. The same callousness and shift are seen when Electra and Orestes trap Aegisthus at his sacrifice (*El.* 619–40, 774–843) and Clytemnestra through her maternal feeling (640–70, 998–1141); and, devastatingly, in Dionysus' treatment of Pentheus – and Cadmus and Agave – in *Bacc.* Similar movements in the audience are started when Theseus believes the dead Phaedra's written incrimination of Hippolytus (*Hipp.* 856–98, 1057–9), which Hippolytus' pride will not let him defend (1060–3, cf. 656–8); or when Hecuba lures the murdering traitor Polymestor to be blinded, by feeding his gold-hunger (*Hec.* 976–1022).[10] In hardly less of a surprise than Creusa's failure in *Ion*, Agamemnon's deception of his wife and daughter is destroyed by their and Achilles' resistance (*IA* 801–1035); it was agony to plan (94–114, cf. 31–42 etc.), and its collapse brings a moral bankruptcy which removes our last sympathy for Agamemnon (1259–75). But Euripides' 'deceptions' extend also to the audience: the slow opening of *HF*, with so much emphasis on the tyrant Lycus, half-creates anticipation that the play will end leisurely with his satisfying destruction; false clues to an action's development are scattered, often in very early scenes, for example when the sleeping Orestes is constantly described as near death (*Or.* 155–210).[11]

Most 'happy endings' stem therefore from external causes or accident, often turned to advantage by human ingenuity. Many readers have seen 'Chance' as the prime mover of many plots, particularly in late Euripides.[12] (But did Euripides use the same order of accident, in the earlier period, to bring Heracles to save Alcestis (*Alc.* 476 ff., 840 ff.); Aegeus to Medea, nursing a miserable childlessness which sparks her infanticide and prompting her request for refuge (*Med.* 663 ff.); or the noble Peleus to save Andromache from the vindictive Hermione and Menelaus (*And.* 547 ff.)?) Others have sought an Aristotelian probability of causation (*Poet.*, esp. 1451a36 ff.) in the intimate realism of so many crucial scenes like 'recognitions' engineered through natural human motive and response (see also below). The rôle of a god, *deus ex machina*, in these endings is also much discussed. There seems now agreement, rightly, that Euripides' *deus* is less a final, all-powerful instrument of rescue 'within the play', than a voice explaining or consoling; or, apparently idiosyncratic to Euripides, which verifies the play's literal outcome through a memory of it perpetuated in cult known to the audience (and, of course, to the mythic account in general). Gods have this 'aetiological' function at the ends of many plays, e.g. *Hipp.* 1423–30, *El.* 1258 ff., *IT* 1449 ff., *Or.* 1646 ff. (*IT* is very clever: the escape-plan is succeeding, when a sudden storm blows the ship back to shore; Athena intervenes, seemingly to secure a second escape, but in the main to assure the would-be captor that the human plan accords with destiny). Where no gods appear, Euripides gives mortals the same mythic clairvoyance, e.g. Medea at *Med.* 1378 ff., Polymestor at *Hec.* 1258 ff., Theseus at *HF* 1328 ff., Oedipus at *Pho.* 1703 ff.[13]

In the more sombre plays, in contrast, choices lead often to unforeseen or harsh consequences: that is a pattern closer to Aristotle's tragic ideal.[14] The taking of known risks, to city as well as self, colours the aid given suppliants in *Hcld.* (236–87) and *Supp.* (337–58, 381–94, 584–97); both plays set the glory of the deed against the unchanging cruelty of war. Euripides' many volunteers for sacrificial death achieve a noble self-fulfilment which lights up in brilliant but poignant contrast the misery (or fortune) of those who live on. Alcestis is the earliest extant example. Polyxena's death is compounded by the discovery of the murdered Polydorus, rousing their broken mother Hecuba to terrible revenge on Polymestor (*Hec.* 670 ff.). Evadne's suicide in her husband's pyre only intensifies her father's desolation (*Supp.* 1094–1107). Erechtheus' daughter dies to save Athens; but she does not save her father in his victory (*Erechtheus* frag. 65.16 ff. Austin). Iphigenia's heroism completes our disgust for Agamemnon.[15]

Phaedra understands and fears her sexual longing (*Hipp.* 373–430), but can only turn on Hippolytus when he rejects it (688 ff.); Hippolytus' avoidance of sex only provokes his destruction through it (99–107, 1400–3) – that is a negative choice, but Pentheus' rejection of Dionysus is aggressive, even if he is unconsciously 'defensive' like Hippolytus. *Med.* and *Hipp.* especially portray the conflict between heart and mind (see § (b) below), which may have controlled some other early plays. At that time Euripides liked women in main parts, 'depraved' or 'wicked' ones like the adulterous Aerope in *Cretan Women* (438), Medea (name-play of 431, but also the murderous deceiver of Pelias in the early *Peliades* of 455), Phaedra (who approached Hippolytus herself in the first version of the play), or Hermione (*And.*, about 425); or 'tragic' or 'unhappy' ones like Hecuba (name-play, about 425), Andromache herself, or Melanippe (two plays of that name, 420s). This last, seduced like so many of Euripides' heroines, and losing or forced to expose her children, later suffered more pain in their refinding: compare Creusa in *Ion*, Hecuba 'recovering' Paris in *Alexandros*, Antiope rescued from torment by her twins in her name-play. Some of these early women are shown in marriage or family settings, where jealousies and wrong-doing are started by improper passions, hard or impossible to contain.

Noteworthy, then, that Euripides continued to favour the 'family' as a *mise-en-scène*, after *Troades*, but for differing purposes. Much tension, but also ethical interest, is generated by his calculated deployment of persons related or closely friendly with one another, especially when they react to predicament, and initiate action, in ignorance of their identities. Sophocles also powerfully exploited familial interaction (for instance, the casting of sisters as foils to Antigone and Electra; the loyalties and disaffections of *Women of Trachis*, *Oedipus at Colonus*), and the family-base of the 'best' tragedy was asserted by Aristotle (*Poet.* 1453a18 ff.) – but Euripides contrived such settings and characters, and their tensions, more consistently and lavishly, especially later: *IT*, *Ion*, *Hel.*, *Pho.*, *Or.*, *Hypsipyle*, *Antiope*, and *IA* stand out.[16] By this means he came to contrast philosophies and styles of life in two stage-persons, where earlier he portrayed conflict and choice inside one person. The contrasts underpin not just show-piece arguments like that between the man-of-action Zethus and his contemplative twin Amphion in *Antiope*, famous in antiquity,[17] but much of a play's whole ethos and movement. *Hipp.* perhaps foreshadows the technique, in Phaedra and Hippolytus; *HF* applies it in Theseus' redemption of Heracles (1214–1426) and *El.* contrasts noble peasant with embittered nobles (1–431); but it flowers in *Pho.*, where Euripides spreads the

contrast of Eteocles and his twin Polynices, through their scenes with
their mother Jocasta and uncle Creon which 'bracket' their verbal
argument (*Pho*. 261–442; 443–637; 690–783), into the long messenger's
report of the battle and their duel (1066–1479); and it is the essence
of *Bacc.* There and elsewhere, complex activity serves as much to expose
the make-up of the agents, as to alter their condition, even in 'happy
endings': Ion 'grows up' in finding himself and his destiny, perhaps,
but Electra and Orestes still need gods to save them from themselves
in *El.* and *Or.*; Artemis may substitute a doe for Iphigenia on the altar
(*IA* 1587 ff. – if the text is Euripides' own), but Agamemnon's misery
remains unchanged since the play's start.[18]

(b) *Mainly on persons; characterization*

Instability, conflict, and change seem to mark many of Euripides'
characters, so that understanding them is problematic. What does it
mean that Aristotle records a *mot* of Sophocles, 'I myself portray men
as they should be, Euripides as they are'? or that Aristophanes has
Euripides attacked for debasing Tragedy with 'low' characters and
Euripides rejoining that they were only everyday figures, easy to
identify with[19] – when neither his contemporaries nor ourselves see
much that is ordinary, within imaginable experience, in their often
extreme situation and behaviour? And did the impact of catastrophe
upon persons, and its theatre, mean more to the poet than their coherent
portrayal, before, during, and after? In point (and often quoted) are
the ancient charges of inconsistency made in the scholion to *Med.* 922
('Medea weeps but still kills her children') and Aristotle, *Poet.* 1454a32
('the Iphigenia who supplicates has no resemblance to the later one':
IA 1246: 1375).

It was an older assumption about Euripides – as about, say, a novel-
ist – that his characters were unitary concepts, whose rounded reconstruction from detail and nuance would unlock one door to a play's total
understanding. Later it was argued that he put the effect of individual scenes before harmonious dramaturgy (and so characterization:
Sophocles was similarly analysed); and that he was mainly interested
in the psychology of separate episodes, causation, course and outcome,
at the cost of consistency.[20] Recent critics concede something to this
last argument, but most insist that the characters remain coherent –
and credible – individuals.

Certain emphases in choice and style of character may relate to phases
in Euripides' work. Plays of the decade centring roughly on the (revised)
Hippolytus of 428 bring their major persons under such pressures, that
instinctive feeling or passion (Greek *thumos*) overcomes any check of
reason (*nous*) and forces a way to its satisfaction past every moral or

physical obstacle. Medea both desires and contrives the first part of her revenge on Jason, the killing of his intended bride, then finds the second part, the infanticide, irresistible to passion and perhaps her own calculation – but she must fight her mother-love to achieve it;[21] Phaedra cannot withstand sexual desire for Hippolytus, but in the hurt pride of rejection destroys them both; Alcmena in *Hcld.* and Hecuba in her name-play are so brutalized by what they undergo that they retaliate in kind.[22] While there is nothing later comparable to the intense power of these characterizations as a 'group', instability or irrationality becomes more marked: Orestes and Electra feel sudden remorse, hard to explain except as dramatic engineering, at the end of *El.* (1177 ff., within 'minutes' of the matricide); Orestes is abruptly persuaded by Pylades to positive resistance (*Or.* 771 ff. – but was Hecuba in her name-play a precedent?); Pentheus capitulates swiftly when Dionysus insidiously invites him to voyeurism (*Bacc.* 800 ff., esp. 810 ff.). It is not quite clear, then, that Euripides is interested in conflict only in earlier plays and instability in later; but he always constructs incident and sequence to dynamize such remarkable changes.

Categorizing the persons by type or function – both are crude criteria – shows that, at any date, Euripides likes the elderly in whom accentuated physical weakness contrasts with unexpected recovery of strength (Iolaus in *Hcld.*, Hecuba in *Hec.*) or with moral assertiveness (Pheres in *Alc.*, Peleus in *And.*; compare Tyndareus in *Or.*, Cadmus in *Bacc.*); or young women who unexpectedly and nobly sacrifice themselves (Macaria in *Hcld.*, Iphigenia in *IA* etc.); or captives whose nobility amid suffering evinces a 'freedom' denied their captors (*And.*, *Hec.*, *Tro.*);[23] or, once more in later plays, characters whose relationship by blood or other intimacy, known, suspected, or rediscovered, galvanizes them to daring (Electra and Orestes in both *El.* and *Or.*, Creusa in *Ion*, Helen and Menelaus in *Hel.* etc.).

Then, may not 'characterization' be something of a misnomer after all? How far is the necessary detail less determined by rôle in a complete action (Aristotle's measure, *Poet.* 1450a15 ff.), than the incidental but cumulative detail is dependent on successive, particular contexts? To allow this effect of the individual scene is not to deny psychological consistency, but to take account of what A. M. Dale, in a seminal and now hallowed phrase, called 'the rhetoric of the situation'. All stage-situations, but particularly the contrast of attitudes in an *agon* ('formal debate'), develop their own momentum, often at the cost of dramatic logic; and persons 'philosophize' implausibly in times of stress which, in detachment, suggest generalizations.[24] But this is how dramatists make action credible, through the words of those who do or experience it; and speech thus mediates character (Aristotle again, *Poet.*

1450a20 ff.). So, it is now well argued, Euripides like all dramatists relies for movement upon his persons' describing their perceptions and desires, and trying to impress them upon others, so that drama shows us pre-eminently figures in 'rhetorical' contexts – contexts, moreover, which in Greek Tragedy are in measure defined by peculiar conventions of theatre, like mask, and of dramatic form and function, like *rhesis* (see § IV(a) below).[25] Despite extremes of predicament and reaction, it may be the everyday-realism, and the familial or friendly intimacy of so many settings, which paradoxically keep the persons within the range of experience and easy identification.[26]

One very new approach seems concerned less to locate characterization within dramatic methods overall, than to suggest for Euripides a unique, precocious ability to project personality and its workings in ways which anticipate modern psychoanalysis. His figures of internal conflict, conscious or unconscious, of violent change, and of abnormality, sometimes perverted, lend themselves to this reading – in particular the agonizing Medea, the sexually tormented Phaedra and the narcissist Hippolytus, and the repressed Pentheus, because of the extent to which Euripides grants them self-examination – and self-deception. The loss of many play-texts (earlier works, mostly) prevents our judging whether he did the same for other deviants whom Aristophanes took as symptomatic of his 'depravity' (see n. 19), e.g. the lustful Stheneboea (name-play, before 430?) or Aerope (*Cretan Women*, 438). I cannot judge professionally such psychoanalyses of the characters, or similar commentaries on their dreams (e.g. *Hec.* 68–97, *IT* 42–60) – but the readings do enlarge my imagination.[27]

NOTES

1. E.g. Lucas, pp. 177–93 and Kitto, pp. 188–90, 250–1 (both admit overlaps); Lesky (1967), p. 137; Schmid, pp. 330–38 (older bibl.). Webster (1967), esp. pp. 31 f., 281, mixes dramatic periods with artificial metrical phases. Similar if not coincident periods in technical development are suggested: see §§ III, IV.

2. Grouped and so called by e.g. Kitto, pp. 311–29; 'romantic tragedy', Conacher, pp. 265–313. For comic elements see Grube, pp. 9–10 etc.; B. M. W. Knox, *Word and Action* (Baltimore, 1979), pp. 250–74.

3. Conacher, pp. 14 f. groups the plays in their attitude to myth and human experience, no patterns of time emerging.

4. See Lesky (1972), p. 381 for other suggested 'trilogies' and Webster (1967), pp. 163 f. on thematic productions generally. G. L. Koniaris, *HSCP* 77 (1973), 85–124 denies thematic connection for the Trojan plays of 415, and demands interpretation of *Tro.* for itself alone.

5. B. M. W. Knox, *YCS* 25 (1977), 197 notes that *Med.* is E.'s only extant play with 'classical' (i.e. Sophoclean) single focus.

6. Unity of *Hec.*: see esp. Conacher, pp. 146–65. *And.*, e.g. P. N. Boulter, *Phoenix* 20 (1966), 51–8 (themes); K. H. Lee, *Antichthon* 9 (1975), 4–16 (thematic and formal elements). Unity in theme: *HF*, e.g. H. H. O. Chalk, *JHS* 82 (1962), 7–18 (virtue, violence, and friendship),

J. W.. Gregory, *YCS* 25 (1977), 259–75 (Heracles' dual fatherhood); *Or.*, W. D. Smith, *Hermes* 95 (1967), 291–307 (disease); *Pho.*, E. Rawson, *GRBS* 11 (1970), 109–27 (family and fatherland).

7. A. Garzya, *Pensiero e Tecnica Drammatica in E.* (Napoli, 1962) finds 'deliverance' as concept and motif determining form in twelve extant plays, *Alc.*, *HF.*, *Med.*, *Hcld.*, *Supp.*, *And.*, *IT.*, *El.*, *Hel.*, *Pho.*, *Or.*, *IA*. A. P. Burnett, *Catastrophe Survived* (Oxford, 1971) takes six of them (*Alc.*, *IT.*, *Hel.*, *And.*, *HF*, *Or.*) and adds *Ion* (and *Cresphontes*) to show how their complex actions trace 'mixed reversals' of fortune; in *CPh* 71 (1976), 4–26 she adds *Hcld.* for its rich mixture of various sub-motifs.

8. 'Suppliant-plays': Strohm, pp. 3–49 ('Agon und Altarmotiv'); Zuntz (1963), pp. 3–54; J. Kopperschmidt, 'Hikesie als dramatische Form', in *Bauformen*, pp. 321–46; cf. Garzya, Burnett in n. 7 above.

9. Sophistication and variation of the dramatic sequence 'ignorance, recognition, intrigue' in the run of plays *El.*, *IT.*, *Ion*, *Hel.*, *Antiope*, *Hypsipyle* were described first by F. Solmsen, *Hermes* 69 (1934), 390–419 (cf. *Philologus* 87 (1932), 1–17). Now, see esp. Strohm, pp. 64–92; Matthiessen, pp. 93–143.

10. *Med.*, *El.*, *Bacc.* are 'revenge-plays' (Lattimore (1964), p. 51 adds *Hcld.*); so certainly is *Hec.* (R. Meridor, *AJP* 99 (1978), 28–35 on Hecuba's duty to avenge Polydorus). Vellacott, p. 226 says 'revenge' is the theme of all plays between *Alc.* and *Hel.* But *Bacc.* also shows 'divine punishment' (with uniquely human agent, A. P. Burnett, *CPh* 65 (1970), 15–29), like *Hipp.*; *Tro.* (1–97) implies it. For 'reversals' as a plot-style, cf. n. 7.

11. Falsehood and deception in the plays: S. Jaekel, *Arctos* 11 (1977), 15–40. For 'red herrings' see esp. W. G. Arnott, *Mus.Phil.Lond.* 3 (1978), 1–14 (bibl.); R. Hamilton, *AJP* 99 (1978), 277–302 (*Ion*, *IT*, *Hel.*, *Alc.*).

12. Circumstance and accident, and human endeavour to surmount them, are thematic: e.g. Lesky (1967), p. 187; (1972), pp. 424–5; Burnett (n. 7 above), pp. 67 ff., esp. n. 19; cf. Conacher, pp. 17 ff. Schmid, p. 702 n. 4 and Webster (1967), p. 287 n. 16 (both give bibl.) deny to E. the fully conceived Hellenistic 'god' Tyche ('Chance'); cf. in § V below.

13. *Deus* and aetiology, cult: Webster (1967), pp. 290 f., cf. ('aesthetic/ritual') Murray, pp. 144–8; A. Spira, *Untersuchungen zum Deus ex machina bei E.* (diss. Frankfurt, 1960) (praised by e.g. Lloyd-Jones, p. 155), but his view of the *deus* as a 'theodicy' is generally rebutted: see Lesky (1972), pp. 518 f. (evaluative bibl.); cf. in general Kitto, pp. 284–7, Grube, pp. 73–9, Strohm, pp. 151–5.

14. Cf. Lattimore (1964), pp. 28–55.

15. For this favourite motif and *coup* see esp. J. Schmitt, *Freiwilliger Opfertod bei E.* (Giessen, 1921); Strohm, pp. 50–63. Cf. Kitto, pp. 254–9; Webster (1967), pp. 103 f., 279; Vellacott, pp. 178–204.

16. Webster (1967), p. 280 stresses 'naturalistic' causation and pp. 287–9 the 'family'; earlier, Strohm, pp. 147 ff. had brought out this 'ethical' quality in later plays.

17. Antiope, frags. IV–XXVI ed. Kambitsis, cf. his pp. XXII–XXX. For bibl. see esp. Snell (1964), pp. 70–98, revised in (1971), pp. 76–103.

18. See Strohm in n. 16 above.

19. Aristot. *Poet.* 1460b33. Ar. *Frogs* 842, 1063 ff. beggars and 846 cripples (cf. *Ach.* 412 ff., *Peace* 147 f.); 1043 ff., 1050 ff., 1079 (and *Thes.* 544–7) adulteresses; E.'s rejoinder *Frogs* 949 f., 959 ff., 971 ff.

20. Unitary conception still canvassed by e.g. E. M. Blaiklock, *The Male Characters of E.* (Wellington, 1952). Individual scenes: esp. E. Howald, *Untersuchungen zur Technik der eur. Tragödie* (Leipzig, 1914). 'Episodic' psychology: esp. W. Zürcher, *Die Darstellung des Menschen im Drama des E.* (Basel, 1947). Kitto, pp. 252–9 relates quality and consistency of characterization to dominance of theme over persons (early) or to persons embodying the dramatic idea (late). The best history of the discussion begins A. Lesky's important 'Psychologie bei E.', in *Entretiens*, pp. 125–68; cf. his *AAHG* 7 (1954), 147 f.; *Ges. Schriften* (Bern, 1966), pp. 247–63. Good general discussions of characterization by C. Garton, *JHS* 77 (1957), 247–54; G. H. Gellie, *AUMLA* 20 (1963), 241–55; J. Gould, *PCPS* 24 (1978), 43–67 (provoked by P. E. Easterling, *G & R* 20 (1973), 3–19, on Aeschylus). For E. cf. also Jones, pp. 252 ff. (penetration), 273 f. (subjectivity). Cf. nn. 24–27 below.

21. 'Passion and reason', esp. in erotic contexts: Lucas, pp. 178–82; Webster (1967), p. 281; Lesky (1967), pp. 154 f. B. M. W. Knox, *YCS* 25 (1977), 193–225 finds in *Med.* the eruption

of suppressed violence (cf. Alcmena in *Hcld.*, Hecuba too?); for the infanticide see now P. E. Easterling, *ibid.*, 177–91; on the difficult verse *Med.* 1079, and context, cf. § V n. 7 below.

22. I borrow 'brutalized' from Webster (1967), p. 281, who goes too far in extending this character-style into e.g. Iphigenia (*IT*) and Creusa (*Ion*).

23. Extensive lists of dramatic types in Schmid, pp. 765 ff. Voluntary sacrifices: n. 15 above; noble captives, e.g. S. G. Daitz, *Hermes* 99 (1971), 217–26 (on *Hec.*); Lesky (1972), p. 513 n. 6; Vellacott, p. 219; K. Synodinou, *On the Concept of Slavery In E.* (Ioannina, 1977). Slaves 'in the drama' well analysed by H. Brandt, *Die Sklaven in den Rollen von Dienern und Vertrauten bei E.* (Hildesheim, 1973). Cf. § V n. 14.

24. Dale, ed. *Alcestis*, pp. xxii ff., the phrase, p. xxvii; *Coll. Papers*, pp. 139–55 ('Ethos and Dianoia'), esp. 150 ff., and pp. 272–80 ('The Creation of Dramatic Characters'). Cf. e.g. Kitto, pp. 256 f., Walcot, pp. 59 ff., Jones, pp. 260 f.

25. See esp. Webster (1967), p. 289 n. 19 and Gould (n. 20 above), with bibl.; earlier e.g. Murray, pp. 131–5, 159 f.

26. E.g. Lattimore (1958), pp. 105 ff., Lucas, pp. 230–32, Webster (1967), pp. 287 ff.; H. Diller in *Entretiens*, pp. 89–121 traces E.'s realism to the clear appreciation by his characters of their place in the dramatic environment. Cf. n. 16 above.

27. A good survey of these readings by C. Segal, *CW* 72 (1978), 129–50. Examples: W. Sale, *YCS* 22 (1972), 63–82 (Pentheus), cf. his *Existentialism in E.* (Victoria, 1977) (*Med., Hipp., Bacc.*); A. V. Rankin, *Arethusa* 7 (1974), 71–94 and J. J. Smoot, *Arethusa* 9 (1976), 37–51 (Hippolytus). G. Devereux, *JHS* 90 (1970), 35–48 (psycho-clinical interpretation of Cadmus with Agave, *Bacc.* 1230 ff.); *Dreams in Greek Tragedy* (Oxford, 1976), esp. pp. 257–318.

III. FORM AND MODE (1): ACTION, EPISODE, THEATRE

(a) *Action and Episode*

The supposedly 'classical' sequence: prologue (or prologue-scene) – *parodos* (entry-song of the chorus) – five episodes, each followed by a choral ode (*stasimon*) – *exodos* (exit-scene): is found in only four plays, *Alc.*, *Med.*, *HF*, *Bacc.* – and only in *Antigone* and *Oedipus at Colonus* of Sophocles, nowhere in Aeschylus.[1] In most plays the fifth episode doubles as the *exodos*; in *Tro.* and *IT* the fourth does (as in all Aeschylus' tragedies except *Agamemnon*). Such external shaping may suggest that Euripides deliberately has fewer main movements than practice, if not tradition, allowed. That is only crudely true. Rather, he both lengthens his episodes, and tends to multiply their internal scenes (best defined by entrances and exits); some scenes are almost independent, so that 'episode' nears 'act' in our sense, and more than one significant development occurs within it. A good example is the very long second episode of *Or.* (356–806, five scenes): Menelaus, Orestes, Tyndareus, and Pylades successively enter, Tyndareus and Menelaus go out in its course; Orestes moves through hope of help from Menelaus, bitter attack from Tyndareus, rejection from Menelaus to a fresh resolution of defiance together with Pylades. In an earlier play the *agon* of Orestes and Tyndareus for Menelaus' approval might well have engrossed a whole episode: so, e.g., Peleus and Menelaus in front of Andromache, *And.* 547–765, or the *agon* of Jason and Medea, *Med.* 446–626. The *Or.*-episode also illustrates the greater number of characters in later plays: the whole drama is richer, more diverse in pressures as well as action.

Euripides begins all his plays with a long 'orientating' prologue-speech, by god (e.g. *Alc.*, *Tro.*) or human character, major (e.g. *Hcld.*) or minor (e.g. *Med.*): some are delivered to the audience alone (e.g. *Bacc.*), some to other persons who hear but do not interrupt (e.g. *Hcld.*, *And.* and other plays beginning with 'tableau'-like ensembles, some including the chorus: *Supp.*). In the prologue-sequence the long speech is followed not by the formal *parodos* (this only in *Supp.* and *Bacc.*, in fact), but by a dialogue (e.g. *Alc.*, *El.*, *HF*) or, increasingly, sometimes additionally, a lyric exchange which introduces the protagonist emotionally: he may share scene and song with the entering chorus (e.g. *Med.*, *Hcld.*, *El.*, *IT*, *Hel.*, *Pho.*) or actually arrogate its start in solo, pathetic anapaests or full monody (e.g. *Hec.*, *Ion*, *Tro.*, *El.*).[2] The breaking of the formal divide here between spoken episode and lyric matches Euripides' tendency everywhere, creating striking dramatic and theatrical continuities and yet variable emotional registers across episodes; at a play's start, it gives pace and interest. At the same time he seems to like containing some formal units, such as monologue, messenger-speech, *agon*, or monody, within their own dynamic and ethical boundaries; but there is seldom tension between them, a kind of war for independence. While they are separable, in the general clarity of episode-structure, and Euripides sometimes openly signals their start and finish (esp. in an *agon*, e.g. *Or*. 491 and 630–1 again), he somehow carries off the illusion that a whole sequence of such units is organically one – this most convincingly in the longer, more various episodes of the later plays.

The last episode and the *exodos* are sometimes fused (above), sometimes formally separated by *stasimon* or lamentatory exchange. They regularly contain the catastrophe, enacted off-stage and reported in a messenger-speech; the subsequent disclosure of the victims, dead or living still to endure (e.g. *Med*. and, supremely, *Bacc*.); and an *envoi* of grief or bitterness, or of explanation, consolation, or reconciliation sometimes worked by Euripides' favourite *deus ex machina*. Once again he early on has simpler effects: a pure *exodos* in *Med*., e.g., when Medea with the children's bodies rides in the Sun-chariot high above the helpless Jason; the dying Hippolytus pardons his father amid Artemis' chilly comfort as she forecasts his cult. Yet even in the early plays the ends of *Alc*. (Heracles restoring Alcestis to Admetus) and *Hcld*. (Alcmena's vindictive assault on Eurystheus) foreshadow in their fresh activity the later move to longer, busy sequences in which episode and *exodos* merge: e.g. at *Hel*. 1512 ff. the messenger reports to Theoclymenus that Helen and Menelaus have escaped, and the king's order of pursuit is stopped short by the Dioscuri as *dei*; *Or*. 1549 ff. has Menelaus on the ground, Orestes, Electra, Pylades, and the hostage Hermione (these three now played by mutes) on the roof of the burning palace, all interrupted by Apollo with the gods' provision. *IA* and *Bacc*., however, revert to the quieter pattern.

In early plays an unexpected and critical turn is often realized by the advent of a 'rescuer' (Heracles in *Alc*., Aegeus in *Med*., Peleus in *And*.) or avenger or destroyer in mid-play, usually the third episode (Theseus in *Hipp*., Heracles in *HF*). The critical development keeps that place in later plays, particularly those of intrigue, where the second and third episodes tend to great length: e.g. *Or*. above, the advent of Menelaus and Tyndareus; *IT* 467–1088, second of four episodes, in which Iphigenia and Orestes are united and plan escape; or *Hel*. 528–1106, third episode of five, in which Helen and Menelaus are united and secure Theonoe's help.[3]

Many analysts find symmetrical or concentric balancing of episodes: in early plays quantitatively, with equivalence in length; in later, also a kind of symbolic bracketing of the long, critical episode at the play's heart: thus, in the early *Med.*, first episode Creon, second Jason, third Aegeus-scene, the 'hinge' of the play, fourth (report of) Creon's death, fifth Jason; or, in the late *Bacc.*, second episode Pentheus captures Dionysus, third the first messenger-speech and the persuasion of Pentheus by Dionysus, fourth Dionysus 'captures' Pentheus. Some patterns claimed are too elaborate and fanciful, but many are indisputable;[4] and the symmetries seem to stand with others of structure and effect, for example in dialogue (see § IV(a) below), so that the poet has presumably some purpose with them. Aesthetic and intellectual self-gratification, only? A response, conscious or not, to canons of proportional beauty in arts like sculpture, architecture? Or a subtle but true means of expression, letting such correspondences and balances not only piece out the whole action clearly, but emphasize the thoroughness of the contrasts, often reversals, they embody? How much of them did the original audience perceive and interpret, how much depends on the reading of a text? That question constantly recurs in Euripides, and imperils many interpretations of his methods and meaning.

(b) *Theatre*

(I assume knowledge of the fifth-century theatre in its basic structure: *orchêstra* ('dance-place'), with side-entrances; accessible from it, the 'stage' and its back-cloth (*skênê*), with central door to an interior, and supports for actors 'on the roof'.[5])

Theatrical facilities and practices were no less historically determined than Tragedy's other modes with which they developed in harmony. Masks; the limit to three of speaking actors; the devices, improbably 'unrealistic' to us, of the wheeled platform which exposed interior scenes through the door (*ekkyklêma*), and of the 'machine' which swung aerial, supernatural visitants into view – such phenomena require the same freedom from prejudicial modern comparisons as do choral dance-song with its stanzaic patterns, or messenger-speech.[6] Euripides' theatre nonetheless shares with our own the representation of credible human beings, however extreme their predicaments: they feel, think, talk, hold themselves and move, doing the actions and gestures of their time, some unique to it, some universally human and so out of time, because that is how Euripides, how any dramatist, conveys reality.

The theatre for which Euripides wrote was essentially the same in its provisions as for Aeschylus; but the *ekkyklêma* and the machine probably came in after Euripides began.[7] He uses no movable resources unavailable to Aeschylus, or Sophocles, like furniture or vessels or stage-extras; nor increases the fluidity of movement between *orchêstra* and *skênê*: so (to illustrate summarily) altars or shrines provide asylum A. *Supp.* 188 ff., *Eum.* 242, 439 ff.; E. *And.* 44, *Supp.* 32 f.; objects focus action and meaning A. *Ag.* 956 f. (the purple cloths), S. *Phil.* 762 ff. (Heracles' bow); E. *Hipp.* 856 f. (Phaedra's tablet), *Bacc.* 1165 ff. (Pentheus' head); persons enter the *orchêstra* by chariot (how drawn? we may assume live animals) and may enter the *skênê* A. *Pers.* 150 ff. (see 607 f.), *Ag.* 906; E. *El.* 998, *Tro.* 569, *IA* 599; persons move between *orchêstra* and *skênê* A. *Pers.* 909 ff., *Cho.* 22 ff., S. *OC* 826; E. *Hipp.* 108, *Hec.* 59 ff., *HF* 529; secondary choruses augment effect A *Eum.* 1006; E. *Hipp.* 54 ff., *Supp.* 1114 ff.; mutes at S. *El.* 16, 1373 (Pylades); E. *El.* 82 (Pylades), *Or.* 1567 (Hermione and Pylades, probably Electra too). It is rather Euripides' busier use of the resources, and his livelier visual sense, which mark him out.

His theatrical style was as readily caricatured by Aristophanes as other idiosyncrasies – although it is worth remembering that Aeschylus was no less powerful scenically, and that even 50 years of death did not save him either from Aristophanes' wit: *Frogs* 832 ff., 911 ff. evoke his notoriously immobile and silent figures. The repeated and extensive parody of whole scenes, like the ragged Telephus of the name-play (438 B.C.) seizing a baby as hostage for his own life (esp. *Acharnians* 280–625, of 425 B.C.; *Thes.* 209–764, of 411), or 'Echo' answering Andromeda's monody and Perseus' arrival to rescue her (*Andromeda*, 412 B.C.: *Thes.* 1009–1135, of 411; Aristophanes has the flying Perseus on the machine, but did Euripides use it?) – these parodies suggest what was felt to be distinctive, if not aggressively new, then, and seems clear to us too. Euripides' realism of incident and detail is calculated for immediacy, but also for effect worked by successive, often climactic, scenic strokes, *coups de théâtre*. Some are briefly or suddenly prepared, like Medea's triumphant escape on her chariot ('machine' *Med.* 1321–2) or Evadne's ecstatic appearance and suicide from the cliff into the pyre, *Supp.* 980–1071 (she leapt from view behind the *skênê*, the only violent 'death on stage' in extant Tragedy[8]); some climax a long sequence, already full of surprises, like the roof-scene ending *Orestes*, after the ins-and-outs of the palace by the plotters and by the demented, effeminate Phrygian, when Apollo stops the murder of Hermione amid the flames, 1246–1693. Small details give vivid colour: Telephus puts on rags, but Menelaus has lost his shirt in the shipwreck, *Hel.* 416–24; Electra's water-jar emphasizes her menial life, *El.* 55, 108, 140; recognition-scenes employ memories or tokens (perhaps over-scrupulously), e.g. *El.* 487–584, *Ion* 1320–1444, and have plausible causation, *IT* 578–826 (Electra's catalytic 'letter home' is praised by Aristotle, *Poet.* 1455a16 ff.). Euripides knows the implication of grouped figures, like menacing initial tableaux with suppliants surrounded at altars (*Hcld.*, *And.*, *Supp.*, *HF* – and Electra with chorus vigilant over the bed-ridden Orestes, *Or.*); and the pathos of funeral procession (*Alc.* 233 ff., *And.* 1166, *Supp.* 794, 1114; the little Astyanax dead upon his father's shield, *Tro.* 1120, 1136 ff.). He exploits the contrast of physical levels to compound meaning: gods announce their higher provision literally, at play-end usually, above the *skênê* from a place conventional for them (*theologeion*, 'where the god speaks')[9]; Jason cannot reach Medea *Med.* 1317 ff., Iphis Evadne *Supp.* 1038 ff., or Menelaus Orestes *Or.* 1567 ff. He shrewdly excites the imagination but more powerfully withholds visible enactment: his favourite, voluntary self-sacrifices are atmospherically prepared but reported in messenger-speech, e.g. Polyxena in *Hec.* or Iphigenia in *IA* (the Cassandra-scene in *Tro.* and Evadne in *Supp.* are demonstrative variations); he threatened aesthetic convention, and heart-attacks for his audience, when in the lost *Cresphontes* Merope was only just stopped, on open stage, from axing her son in ignorance (Aristot. *Poet.* 1454a5; Plut. *Mor.* 998E). He uses the tension between visible scene and invisible interior dexterously: Phaedra overhears Hippolytus repudiating the Nurse, *Hipp.* 565 ff.; the Chorus hear Polymestor's blinding, *Hec.* 1035 ff.; Dionysus inside the palace commentates his own miraculous assault on it, *Bacc.* 576–603 (there was also a simulated earthquake in the lost *Erechtheus*) – and then the impact of the off-stage action is continued in its subsequent exposure: Polymestor stumbles from the tent, groping for Hecuba who blinded him; Heracles bound to a pillar amid the children he has killed is drawn out on the *ekkyklêma* (*HF* 1028 ff.), after the chorus outside have heard Amphitryo inside trying to prevent him (887–909; messenger's report in between, 910–1015).[10]

Illustration imperils useful generalization, as always; some of the scenes cited slightly misrepresent Euripides' preference for depicting reaction rather than action (this is true even for large parts of the 'melodramatic' *IT*, *Hel.*, and *Ion*). He concentrates upon aftermath, in suffering, grief, bitterness. *Med.*, *Hipp.*, *And.*, *Hec.*, *Supp.*, *HF*, *Tro.*, *El.*, *Pho.*, *Or.*, and *Bacc.* show why, in the properly tragic extrapolation of catastrophe which ends his plays, Aristotle excused Euripides his other dramatic faults (*Poet.* 1453a28 ff.).[11]

NOTES

N.B. Almost all the main advances in studying Tragedy's formal structures have been made by German scholarship, which the Notes in this and the next section cannot conceal. Murray, pp. 131–60 and Lattimore (1964), pp. 14 f., 56–72 discuss form and convention in poetic drama sensitively; cf. Greenwood, pp. 128–41, Grube, pp. 24–8.

1. The five-'act'-structure becomes regular only in Tragedy's post-'classical' beneficiary, New Comedy: R. T. Weissinger, *A Study of Act Division in Classical Drama* (Iowa City, 1940).

2. H. W. Schmidt, 'Die Struktur des Eingangs', in *Bauformen*, pp. 1–46, subsumes and develops all earlier studies of prologue-speech, -scene and *parodos* (bibl. in his p. 1 f., nn. 4.6; cf. Schmid, pp. 771–5). See esp. M. Imhof, *Bemerkungen zu den Prologen der soph. und eur. Tragödien* (Winterthur, 1957); F. Stoessl, 'Parodos', *RE* 23.I, 632–41; 23.II, 2312–45. Grube, pp. 63–73 and 107–110 (*parodoi*) gives the best English survey; cf. Murray, pp. 135–7, Kitto, pp. 278–84.

3. There are statistical and analytic synopses of episode and scene, in relation to plot, by K. Aichele, 'Das Epeisodion', in *Bauformen*, pp. 47–83 (esp. 61 f., 73–9 for E., with bibl. at 73 nn. 73 and 74). Excellent comparative appreciations in e.g. Friedrich, Matthiessen, Ludwig (pp. 93–138) and esp. Strohm (pp. 165–82), who stresses fluency; in English, Grube, pp. 80–92.

4. For the patterns in *Med.* see e.g. Strohm, pp. 168 f., Aichele, p. 62, in *Bacc.* Strohm, p. 180, Aichele, pp. 62 f. – and Taplin (1978), pp. 138 f., the end of a chapter which establishes persuasively the real effect of 'mirror-scenes'. Webster (1967), pp. 282 f. is sceptical of such symmetries, but also recognizes patterns. While Ludwig showed the clear structure and proportions of later plays, both he and some followers have gone too far in finding symmetries: Friedrich (e.g. pp. 16 ff. on *Ion*, 73 ff. on *Tro.*), Matthiessen and Strohm use the undeniable evidence most sensitively.

5. Excellent, lively introduction by Taplin (1978), esp. pp. 1–21 (fuller on the resources, with bibl., (1977), pp. 434–51); also P. D. Arnott, *Introduction to the Greek Theatre* (London, 1959). pp. 1–62; H. C. Baldry, *The Greek Tragic Theatre* (London, 1971), pp. 1–73. For other works see n. 10 below.

6. Necessary warnings well stated by the writers named in n. 5 and esp. Greenwood, pp. 121 ff., Walcot (early chapters).

7. Evidence and conjecture assessed by Taplin (1977), pp. 442–7.

8. For Ajax's suicide in Sophocles, see P. D. Arnott, *Greek Scenic Conventions in the Fifth Century B.C.* (Oxford, 1962), pp. 131–8 and Lesky (1972), p. 191. Cf. Taplin (1978), p. 189 n. 5.

9. Elsewhere in plays: Iris and Madness at *HF* 815 ff., probably Aphrodite at *Hipp.* 1 ff. (to balance Artemis at the end, whose high place is implicit in Hippolytus' vagueness at 1391–3 and her own spiritual coldness). Only Thetis at *And.* 1228 and the Dioscuri at *El.* 1233 use the 'machine': see Barrett, ed. *Hippolytos*, p. 397 f. Gods in prologues normally use the ground: Apollo and Death in *Alc.*, Dionysus certainly in *Bacc.* (see 47–54); Poseidon and Athena in *Tro.*, too, probably.

10. The best collective treatments of evidence, archaeological and literary (esp. the plays!), are R. C. Flickinger, *The Greek Theater and its Drama* (Chicago, 1936⁴); A. W. Pickard-Cambridge, *The Theatre of Dionysus at Athens* (Oxford, 1947) and *The Dramatic Festivals of Athens* (2. ed. by J. Gould, D. M. Lewis, Oxford, 1968); T. B. L. Webster, *Greek Theatre Production* (London, 1970²). For appreciation of the resources *in use* see esp. Taplin's books (bibl.); Arnott (n. 8 above); N. C. Hourmouziades, *Production and Imagination in E.* (Athens, 1965); Steidle, esp. pp. 9–25. Kitto, pp. 272–8, however, thinks that E.'s bold theatre often masks dramatic weakness.

Some special discussions: Dale, *Coll. Papers*, pp. 119–29, 259–71 (off-stage action; *ekkyklêma*); K. Joerden, 'Zur Bedeutung des Ausser- und Hinterszenischen', in *Bauformen*, pp. 369–412 (bibl.); J. Dingel, *Das Requisit in der griechischen Tragödie* (diss. Tübingen, 1967) (cf. *Bauformen*, pp. 347–67); A. Spitzbarth, *Spieltechnik der griechischen Tragödie* (Zurich, 1946) (useful *index locorum*); D. Bain, *Actors and Audience* (Oxford, 1977) devotes pp. 13–66 to 'asides' in E.; D. J. Mastronarde, *Contact and Discontinuity: Some Conventions of Speech and Action on the Greek Tragic Stage* (Berkeley, 1979); R. Hamilton, 'Announced Entrances in Greek Tragedy', *HSCP* 82 (1978), 63–82; D. Stanley-Porter, 'Mute actors in the tragedies of E.', *BICS* 20 (1973), 68–93.

Mary Renault's novel *The Mask of Apollo* (London, 1966) wonderfully – and accurately – evokes an actor's life in the fourth century.

11. J. de Romilly, *L'évolution du pathétique d'Eschyle à Euripide* (Paris, 1961) stresses the predominantly pathetic mode; cf. Jones, p. 267. P. Pucci, *The Violence of Pity in E.'s Medea* (Cornell U. P., 1979) writes on E.'s "remedial" 'rhetoric of pity and fear' (cf. his *Arethusa* 10 (1977), 165–95). For Tragedy's immediacy of emotional experience, then and now, see esp. Vickers, pp. 78–96; Taplin (1978), pp. 167–71.

IV. FORM AND MODE (2): SPEECH, SONG, LANGUAGE

(a) *Speech*

To generalize: in Greek Tragedy, lyric, whether song alone or dance-song, voices emotion and registers a mood, collective or personal; speech explains mood, attitude, reaction, intention, or decision, from reason. So movement in the drama occurs predominantly through spoken episode alternating with song.[1] In that, at the start of visible European drama, Tragedy no more than inherits from Epic, which was both 'oral' as a traditional poetry and largely oral in its dramatic narrative: Homer prefers his persons, not himself, to say why and what they did, are doing, and will do.

Within spoken episode, Euripides favours very strongly two forms: the *rhesis*, or individually substantive speech, at least six or seven lines long (briefer ones are either formal announcements or acknowledgements, or interdependent parts of dialogue); and *stichomythia*, dialogue between two, rarely three, persons in which each speaks a single line or half-line or couplet, in turn, in sequences up to a hundred or more lines long.

Free or 'natural' dialogue, exchanging speeches of varying *brevity*, is usually short, a dozen lines or so, e.g. at a messenger's entry *Hipp.* 1153–72, *And.* 1070–84, *Pho.* 1067–89. Greater length is rare, and often excited, e.g. the end of Medea's and Jason's *agon*, Med. 579–626 (9,3,2,5,2,3,2,1,1,1,1,7,3,4,4 speech-lines); or Agamemnon, Hecuba, and Polymestor after the blinded Polymestor's re-entry monody, *Hec.* 1109–31 (5,2,4,2,2,3,1/2,11/2,3), cf. *Hel.* 761–79, *IA* 1098–1128. Such freer dialogue is commonly interrupted by brief *rhesis*: e.g. *Hipp.* 680–731 shows Phaedra, after Hippolytus' rejection, in angry exchange first with Nurse (dismissed 709), then with Chorus – but Phaedra has *rheseis* of 13 lines (682–94), 7 (715–21) and 7 1/2 (724–31); or symmetrical sequences, often stichomythic, invade, e.g. the *agon* of Theseus and Hippolytus, *Hipp.* 1038–89; Orestes' arrival, *And.* 881–920; Hecuba securing Agamemnon's acquiescence, *Hec.* 726–86.

Although the plays tend to lengthen, *rheseis* themselves become neither longer nor more numerous – but stichomythic exchanges do, and seem to take on a more critical role in moving the action forward, embodying discussion or decision for which the preceding *rheseis* prepare.[2] The development reflects Euripides' shift from individual-centred drama of the early period, especially the plays portraying internal conflict, in which *rhesis* dominates. The later plays are more open, their predicaments often externally and fortuitously determined; recognition- and reunion-scenes, and the conception and execution of plans, mostly for revenge or escape, among intimates, make the intense dialogue of *stichomythia* more apt, e.g. in the second episode of *El.*, 487–698, or of *Ion*, 510–675, or the end of that in *Or.*, 725–806.

To categorize *rheseis*, in the way scholars inevitably do, as static (informative, explanatory, self-revelatory), deliberative, or dynamic, is easy enough, but these are no more than orders of dramatic function. It is more useful to know that Euripides demonstrably varies the styling of long speeches for particular contexts. Monologue is a prime example: in the early plays just noticed, soliloquy, but also monologue, conveys intense, anguished self-appeal and self-examination, e.g. *Med.* 214 ff., 1021 ff., *Hipp.* 373 ff., 616 ff., *Hec.* 585 ff. In harmony with the differing general tone of later plays, Euripides favours monologue, especially 'to the chorus', for the disclosure of attitude and deliberation, 'thinking aloud', e.g. *IT* 77 ff., *Hel.* 255 ff. or (before two as yet unnoticed persons) *Bacc.* 215–47; there he made a precedent, and perhaps an influence, for New Comedy's practice.[3] In just this period, too, he begins markedly to prefer monody or lyric exchange, again mostly with the chorus, to monologue or soliloquy, for the revelation of extreme emotion, grief, anguish, or even ecstasy (see § (b), below).

Some other prominent types of *rhesis* have been analysed both in context and as independent structures. First, those in the formal *agon* (e.g. *Alc.* 614–740, *Hipp.* 916–1089, *Hec.* 216–443, *HF* 140–239, 1214–1426, *Or.* 459–724) and in the similarly conceived entreaty-scenes, or confrontations between persecutor and rescuer, of 'suppliant-dramas' (e.g. *Hcld.* 120–287, *And.* 309–463, 547–765, *Supp.* 110–262, 399–584).[4] The internal mechanisms of these strongly combative and pointedly opposed *rheseis* show Euripides realizing vividly, sometimes a little self-indulgently, the potential of 'law-court' drama, rather than demonstrating simply a command of rhetorical technique.[5] Two further types: Euripides controls his favourite, long prologue-speeches by varying factual orientation of the audience with suggestion to their sympathies: *Hipp.* 41 ff. and *Bacc.* 39 ff., both by gods, are good examples, but compare e.g. *IT* 40 ff., *Or.* 52 ff.[6] Messenger-speeches are infinitely more spacious and colourful, but equally well-calculated; simpler in build, usually linear in narrative, their readily comprehensible order of events is never put at risk; variety comes in pace and intensity, as they sometimes slow or stop their camera for the spectator, so that a vignette may suddenly point the whole scene by its very detail.[7] Nearly all the speeches, then, of whatever dramatic function, have a natural, orderly sequence, clear to the audience – even the sometimes tormented early monologues. Only the agonistic *rheseis* abandon naturalism for more calculated effects, like the measured telling-off of arguments to match an opponent's, or digressions, whether illustrative or corroborative, especially in 'proofs' and appeals to general principle.[8]

Dialogue, *stichomythia* above all, easily reveals its structure, and often an astonishing internal symmetry of line-numbers and topics, or stages, a kind of metronomic progression. Dramatic or 'ethical' rationale is not always so evident. The form is superbly apt and effective for tense altercation, before or after an exchange of *rheseis* in an *agon* (e.g. *Alc.* 708 ff., *Hcld.* 253 ff., *Pho.* 588 ff.), or for interrogations which expose the inner person, forcing out reluctant truths (e.g. *Hipp.* 311 ff., *Bacc.* 792 ff.); its surface rigidity is forgotten in excitement. It is hardly less suited for the rapid exchange of information (e.g. *HF* 610 ff., *Supp.* 750 ff.), for persuasion or deception (e.g. *IT* 1153 ff., *Hel.* 1193 ff.) or for the formulation of plans (e.g. *Ion* 970 ff., *Or.* 1100 ff.) – but Euripides frequently uses the form for extended communication of fact, or narration, where a long speech would have served the drama better (e.g. *Supp.* 115 ff., *Ion* 262 ff.); and the length is unrealistic and implausible to us, even if we conspire with its ethos and even if Euripides was successful with his original audience for displaying technical virtuosity. The maintenance of unvarying form does not match the changing direction or stress of the exchange, e.g. in the first meeting of Ion and Creusa, *Ion* 262–368 above, or the protracted sharing of half-lines (*antilabe*) when Xuthus greets his presumed son Ion, 517–65.[9]

It is noteworthy that Euripides only very seldom has three persons in dialogue, and then usually in successive pairings (e.g. *Hcld.* 630–94, *El.* 612–85) or with the third seldom intervening (e.g. *Pho.* 617–25). Sophocles, however, uses three voices quite freely, especially in excited scenes (e.g. *OT* 1110–85, *Phil.* 1288–1313, *OC* 820–47): that freedom goes with the poet's general avoidance of settled stichomythic spans, when he represents much more plausibly the irregularity of speech and feeling.[10]

The verse of Tragic speech is the iambic trimeter, an instrument which Euripides appears to tune with some subtlety. The steady increase throughout his career in the number of long syllables 'resolved' into two shorts, and of other prosodic or rhythmic licences, was observed soon after 1800; it provides the most reliable of internal inferences for the comparative dating of plays where external evidence is lacking. Recent study analyses ever more minutely the relation between 'resolution' and word-shape; between principal caesura and minor divisions in the verse; and between all these and sense-units, small or large, particularly at and across verse-end. An 'aesthetic' *vue d'ensemble* is nevertheless still lacking and a most difficult task, to answer such questions as: does Euripides modulate his trimeter according to ethical context, and even between *rhesis* and dialogue – except in so far as differing diction, and the equivalence of verse with complete sense-unit, probably oblige?[11] Scholarship has something to do there, comparable with its assessment of the other, but much less common, metre of speech, the trochaic tetrameter. Euripides seems to have revived the metre (after Aeschylus' *Persae* and *Agamemnon* it occurs only in the disputed last seven lines of the *Oedipus Tyrannus*), and uses it in all the extant plays after *Tro.*, except *Hel.* and *Ion*. First, it is only for *rheseis*, later also for dialogue, either to mark changes of theme and especially tempo across changes of scene within episodes (e.g. *HF* 855–73, *Bacc.* 604–41) and, especially, for excited or critical moments (e.g. *IT* 1203–33, *IA* 317–401, 855–916, 1338–1401).[12]

(b) *Song*

Euripides varies and experiments with lyric more than Aeschylus or Sophocles, in form and purpose, for choral song; for antiphony within the chorus or with a character or between characters; or for actor's solo.

The importance of the chorus in the drama ranges from whole-hearted participation, as in *Supp.*; profound emotional involvement if less emphasized physical sharing, as in *Tro.* and *Bacc.*; through occasional furtherance of the main action, e.g. at *Hcld.* 101 ff., 271, *IT* 1293 ff., *Or.* 1246 ff., or at least complicity in it, e.g. *Med.* 267 ff., 811 ff., *Hipp.* 891 f., 1036 f.; to neutrality or bystanding, as in *Pho.* (where the chorus are actually heralded at 193–201 as a 'talkative, troublesome crowd of women'!).[13] Whatever their participation, their sympathies are normally evident, and often pronounced; that, and their constant presence, allows their songs, especially the *stasima*, a wide range of effect and mood, in harmony or counterpoint with the action. They reflect directly on what they have heard or seen, or anticipate in hope or anxiety (e.g. *Med.* 976 ff., *Hipp.* 769 f., *Supp.* 375 f.); or they comment allusively, often implicitly, providing from mythic illustration or comparison a wider, universal background to particular predicament, as in the largely thematic odes of *Tro.* (the Paris-story; the Trojan War), or *Pho.* (the Theban past); or they interrupt mood and setting, with contrast or relief, if very seldom breaking the stage illusion entirely.[14]

Amid such variety of function, some habits or trends in form and language at least are visible. In the *stasima*, two pairs of 'responding' strophes are the norm, with or without epodes; a single pair (e.g. *Pho.* 1283–1307, with epode e.g. *And.* 766–801, *Supp.* 955–79) is hardly commoner than three pairs, a limit not exceeded except perhaps at *IA* 164–302 (*parodos*: text uncertain). Comment or illustration normally moves from the general case or the nearer time in the first strophic pair, to the particular case or the remoter time in the second.

'Responsion' between strophe and antistrophe not just of metre, line, or line-group, but also of themes, images, words, phrases – or contrasts of the same – are purposely contrived (*And.* 274–83 = 284–92, 293–300 = 301–8 and *Supp.* 955–62 = 963–70 illustrate most of these symmetries). *Stasima* nevertheless tend to increase in length, and metrical freedom and complexity: that change goes with an apparent shift from lyric extension or comment on the preceding episode, to the indirect, oblique bearing on the action, even independence, just noted. In the latest plays narrative *stasima* (and monodies: see below) appear, aptly called 'dithyrambic' from their lush diction, tortuous style, and exotic rhythms. It is likely that Euripides embraced a vogue for such 'new music' about this time, represented for us only in the surviving large fragment of his friend Timotheus' dithyrambic poem *Persae*, composed soon after 420.[15] Some of these later odes especially earned Aristotle's censure as inorganic, symptomatic of a growing fashion for choral songs which were mere lyric *intermezzi*, a fashion neither Tragedy nor Comedy in the fourth century resisted (*Poet.* 1456a27 ff.).

Only one *stasimon* is antiphonal between two semi-choruses (*Supp.* 598–633), but the chorus quite often divides for a greater dynamic of emotion outside *stasima*, e.g. *Alc.* 77 ff. (*parodos*), 213–37, *Hipp.* 362–72, *HF* 875–84 etc.; at *Or.* 1246 ff. it begins an exchange with Electra as a unit, and from 1258 continues it in semi-chorus.

Other lyrics become even more fluid. Formal *stasima* are often supplemented or replaced by lyric exchanges (*amoibaia*), in which the chorus sometimes plays little part, only punctuating a lyric solo or duet from the actors. The varieties of form may seem bewildering (there are over fifty *amoibaia* extant), but again some trends are visible. Antiphonies of grief are appropriately expressed in strophic form, with close 'responsion' of the voice-parts and sometimes also of sense- and sound-units; these are commoner in early plays, e.g. *And.* 1197–1225, *Supp.* 1123–64. So too are 'epirrhematic' *amoibaia*, in which one voice speaks or perhaps intones iambic trimeters alternately with a lyric voice (or two), e.g. *Alc.* 244–79 (strophic exchange, after a *stasimon*), *Hcld.* 73–110 (strophic; = *parodos*), and (all 'astrophic', i.e. without stanzaic shape) *Hipp.* 565–95 following a *stasimon*; *Tro.* 239–91; *Pho.* 103–92 preceding *parodos* of the chorus. Peculiarly Euripidean are the gradual displacement of strophic by astrophic form in these exchanges, and increasing invasion by the solo voice; sometimes it prefaces the exchanges, especially in the long, complex structures preferred for the *parodos*, from as early as *Med.* 96–213; then e.g. *Hec.* 59–215, *El.* 112–212, *Ion* 82–237.[16]

Career-long experimentation found one very vivid, we might fairly say, theatrical, form of lyric expression, the monody. It appears in

all the plays except *Med.*, *HF*, and *Bacc.* (where its denial to Agave
is striking); in fact the early *Hipp.* has three monodies, and *Hec.* four.
The latest plays use the form most (both *Hel.* and *Pho.* have four and
there are fragments from the late *Andromeda* and *Hypsipyle*); and here
it is longest and rhythmically most unrestrained, and achieves the
greatest independence, e.g. *Ion* 859–922, *Or.* 1369–1502, *IA* 1279–1335.
Its largely reactive rôle and anguished, often despairing mood suggest
that it emerged from the *amoibaion* of grief, the *kommos*. It may be
significant that most of the early monodies are strophic (like the greater
part of Sophocles' five: Aeschylus has none at all, but the *Prometheus*
two, astrophic); perhaps strophic form intended some kind of poignant
contrast between external show and internal turbulence, or even irony.
Just one or two monodies are prospective, sometimes ecstatically so,
even if of death (Evadne at *Supp.* 990 ff., Cassandra at *Tro.* 308 ff.;
Jocasta at *Pho.* 301–54 uniquely mixes joy with fear). Euripides chooses
the persons for his monodies with great care, in relation to the whole
play's casting and theme; he seldom imperils the prominence they give
a major figure by having a minor figure also sing (but note Ion and
Creusa in *Ion*). Still, it is striking that the majority of monodists are
women, and that only Hippolytus (1347–88) and Ion (82–183) of the
males are major figures. The wording of monodies implies strongly
theatrical performance – Evadne in her blind transport of ecstatic grief
hangs on the cliff-edge before her suicide; the demented Phrygian
'narrates' the mayhem he has escaped (*Or.* 1369–1502). All these
qualities called for virtuoso acting, and the form shows Euripides at
his most daring and demanding.[17]

(c) *Language*

Ancient critics praised the naturalness of Euripides' spoken verse,
effective and pleasing to the ear through its skilful composition from
ordinary language; fluent from the smooth interweaving of manageable
units of sense and rhythm. Clarity of diction indeed characterizes his
rhesis, and straightforwardness, so that it often achieves an unaffected
dignity, of statement or feeling. Good examples are Alcestis' words
before death *Alc.* 280–325, Andromache's appeal to Menelaus *And.*
384–420, Heracles' capitulation to Theseus *HF* 1340–93, Cadmus'
dismay *Bacc.* 1302–26.[18]

Antiquity was also attracted by the 'rhetorical' quality which made
Euripides a favourite set-book: he was rich in moral or philosophical
ideas and illustrative generalizations, clever and striking in their
deployment.[19] These can occur without special dramatic need or con-
textual aptness; instances almost notorious are Hecuba's disquisition
upon inherited virtue and education in the apostrophe of her dead

daughter at *Hec.* 591 ff., and Orestes musing on the relation between status and virtue at *El.* 367 ff. They occur above all where whole or part-episodes depend upon contrast of attitude, argument or appeals both rational and impassioned; the *agon* is the chief place. Nineteenth-century scholarship created a barrier to grasping style and purpose by classifying organization and figures too nicely with labels, as if the poet had been primarily and systematically a rhetorician in the empty sense, for whom manipulation of language was all-important. The twentieth century has found a truer perspective.[20] Euripides' rhetorical quality is real, and marked, even idiosyncratic; but it is only one means among many of formulating, most readily to his own habits of thought and experience as a 'modern' intellectual, the tensions of his stage-world – a world whose persons and predicaments he tried to make immediate and accessible to his contemporary audience by expressing myth in contemporary idiom. We must balance particularly our modern sensitivity to 'rhetorical' styling against awareness of other modes: simple dramatic context and theme, pressure and reaction, intention and obstacle in the identity of stage-persons, their theatrical bearing and gesture, and so on. It needs to be said that rhetorical figures and speeches seem more obvious in the original Greek than in translation, perhaps because English (at least) is itself less 'formal'.

Rhetoric (and there is no better one-word term) by its nature is commoner in long speeches, but the dominant impression is still of fluent clarity. Naturalness *in language* survives also the superficially crippling constraint of *stichomythia*, helped by a truly virtuoso technique which controls pace, point, and nuance through overlap of the verse-unit by syntax or sense; judicious repetition of words or ideas, or their subtle variation in synonym; and finely weighed choice of particles, to us the most elusive of tonal devices. Euripides shows these skills from the start (indeed they are already evident in the terse *stichomythiae* of Aeschylus); the earliest of the following examples is as accomplished as the latest: *Alc.* 1077 ff., *Hipp.* 311 ff., *Supp.* 566 ff., 1048 ff., *IT* 492 ff., *Bacc.* 923 ff.[21]

The lyric style, in contrast, both choral and monodic, grows increasingly exotic. The simple colours and decoration of the early plays give way to ornament, with detail, images and sound overworked in such phenomena as proliferation of epithets; verbs and adjectives profusely coined, often merely with variant suffixes; apparently random doubling of words ('emotional' emphasis?); chains of participles and clauses. Many of these lyric effects are lost in translation, but compare the directness of e.g. *Med.* 976–1001 (the chorus forecast death for Jason's bride) or even Hecuba's and Polyxena's agonized songs at *Hec.* 154–74, 197–215, with the lush extravagance of e.g. *Pho.* 202–60 (*parodos*) or 1485–1538 (Jocasta's monody). These are extremes, certainly, but the same poet did write both, in a development consistent with his other musical and metrical experimentation. The easy but brilliant parodies by Aristophanes of Euripides' lyric style must indicate at the least discomfort, if not offence, among his contemporaries.[22]

Individual components of language and style, particularly lyric, have been studied thoroughly. Again, the nineteenth century looked mainly at *minutiae*, pinning them like butterflies, but the twentieth century too has categorized and listed exhaustively.[23] Recent interest is healthily in broader tones and colours, and qualities of diction derived and invented. Critical synthesis is attempted, so that we are not only informed about the poetic (or everyday) pedigree of all vocabulary, figures, and sound-effects, but have the basis for a better *general* appreciation, from context to context.

Two prime examples. Colloquialisms give nuance to moments of dialogue, also of *rhesis* (and occur sporadically in lyric); Euripides uses them regularly for both heroic and humbler persons, consistently with the general egalitarianism of his stage (unlike Aeschylus or Sophocles).[24] Imagery receives the most fruitful appreciation, for it is manifold and subtle.[25] Single images, or simile and metaphor, may illuminate character and emotion, helping to fix tone and mood: Hecuba invites the listener to stand back from her grief and contemplate it in its fullness as a painter does his work, *Hec.* 807 f.; Pentheus imagines himself coming upon the maenads, catching them in the act of love like birds in a thicket, *Bacc.* 957 f. Images become thematic in a play, like the sea in *IT* or the mountains in *Bacc.*: thus ocean, woodland, and meadow pervade *Hipp.* in the longings and experience of Phaedra and Hippolytus (note the identical eroticism of the 'virgin' meadow possessively evoked by Hippolytus, 73–8, and Phaedra in her fantasy, 208–11); confusion of light and darkness in the spoken imagery of Pentheus and Dionysus supports 'stage-effects' like the double sun (*Bacc.* 918) in the drama of their conflict.[26] Some images are both thematic and individually emphatic, like the much-cited picture of Megara's children as helpless boats-in-tow, *HF* 629–33, 1423–4, cf. 478–9 – and the analogous trace-horses 445–6.[27] Rich, often intricate imagery calls up landscapes of nature or human experience, and of intense feeling, above all in choral ode and monody: good examples are the superb songs of *Bacc.*; the chorus' apostrophe of Troy now devastated (e.g. *Tro.* 511 ff., 1060 ff.) or its reflections on Paris' Judgement (*And.* 274 ff., *Hec.* 629 ff.);[28] or Ion's monody celebrating Apollo's Delphi (*Ion* 82–183).

NOTES

1. See esp. Taplin (1977), pp. 49–60, 'Action and Formal Structure'; Greenwood, pp. 136–9.

2. Statistical survey by B. Mannsperger, 'Die Rhesis', in *Bauformen*, pp. 143–81, esp. 144–9 (who 143 n. 4 and 168 n. 69 notes that there are no *comprehensive* studies of Tragic rhesis, in contrast with lyric); also B. Seidensticker, 'Die Stichomythie', ibid., pp. 183–220, esp. 209–19.

3. Schadewaldt (esp. pp. 94–262 on E.) remains the major study of monologue, developing for Tragedy F. Leo, *Der Monolog im Drama* (Berlin, 1908).

4. J. Duchemin, *L'Agon dans la tragédie grecque* (Paris, 1968²) offers exhaustive formal analyses; cf. my 'Formal Debates in E.'s Drama', *G & R* 22 (1975), 58–71 (principal bibl. at 59 n. 1). Cf. also § II n. 8 above.

5. For 'rhetoric' in E. see § (c), esp. n. 20 below.

6. Prologue-speeches: Schadewaldt, pp. 6 ff., ('second' prologues, by new entrants) 240 ff.; tone, e.g. Grube, pp. 63–8. Emotionally dramatic: H. Strohm, *GB* 6 (1977), 113–32 (*Alc., Med., And.*, and *Supp.*). Bibl.: Schmid, p. 771 n. 2, Lesky (1972), p. 507 n. 3; cf. n. 2 above.

7. Analyses in J. Keller, *Struktur und dramatische Funktion der Botenberichte bei Aischylos und Sophokles* (diss. Tübingen, 1959); G. Erdmann, *Der Botenbericht bei E.* (diss. Kiel, 1964). Technique and imagery: Barlow, pp. 61–78; general appreciation: Murray, pp. 140–44, cf. J. Bremer, 'Why messenger-speeches?' *Miscellanea Tragica* (*Festschrift* Kamerbeek) (Amsterdam, 1976), pp. 29–48. Bibl.: Schmid, p. 777 n. 4.

8. General assessments of *rhesis* in the drama by Murray, pp. 138–40 and Lattimore (1964), pp. 64–8; more critical of 'rhetoric', Kitto, pp. 265–72.

9. The most useful studies of *stichomythia* are E. R. Schwinge, *Die Verwendung der Stichomythie in den Dramen des E.* (Heidelberg, 1968) (*very* long, over-nice) and B. Seidensticker, *Die Gesprächsverdichtung in den Tragödien Senecas* (Heidelberg, 1969), pp. 19–75 (summarized in *Bauformen*, pp. 183–220). I review these and earlier studies of the form, and its problems, in *LCM* 5 (1980), 77–85 (80 on the remarkable symmetries).

10. Schmid, p. 783 n. 11; G. F. Listmann, *Die Technik des Dreigesprächs in der griechischen Tragödie* (diss. Giessen, 1910); Seidensticker in *Bauformen*, pp. 203 f. (Soph.), 210 f. (Eur.).

11. For the trimeter and the dating of the plays, see § I n. 3. Other main studies: J. Descroix, *Le trimètre iambique* (Mâcon, 1931); pauses: J. D. Denniston, *CQ* 30 (1936), 73–9, 192 and T. C. W. Stinton, *CQ* 27 (1977), 67–72; enjambement: F. Humborg, *Quaestiones Euripideae etc.* (diss. Münster, 1909). C. Prato is trying to answer the questions: see *Ricerche sul trimetro dei tragici greci: metro e verso* (Roma, 1975), esp. pp. 9–16 (bibl.) and 111–230; cf. *QUCC* (1972), 4.73–113 ('resolution' a stylistic device to be assessed in context).

12. T. Drew-Bear, 'The trochaic tetrameter in Greek Tragedy', *AJP* 89 (1968), 385–405 omits M. Imhof, *MH* 13 (1956), 125–43 from his bibl. Summary information in *Bauformen*, pp. 164–7.

13. For the chorus in *Pho.* see esp. Conacher, pp. 245–8.

14. W. Kranz, *Stasimon* (Berlin, 1933) remains the cardinal work on the Tragic chorus. Useful generalizations by J. Rode, 'Das Chorlied', in *Bauformen*, pp. 85–115 (good bibl.). A. M. Dale, 'The Chorus in the Action of Greek Tragedy', *Coll. Papers*, pp. 210–20 is concise. For E. in particular Grube, pp. 99–126 is very balanced and Webster (1967), pp. 283–5 helpful; cf. Murray, pp. 149–58; Kitto, pp. 259–65, 341–6; Vickers, pp. 13–23; C. Möller, *Vom Chorlied bei E.* (diss. Göttingen, 1933); H. Parry, *The Choral Odes of E.* (diss. Berkeley, 1963) (structure and dramatic relevance); G. B. Walsh, *The Relief Odes of E.* (diss. Yale, 1974); R. Padel, *CQ* 24 (1974), 227–41 ('imagery of the elsewhere': mainly *Hipp.* 732–75, *Hel.* 1451–1511); 'thematic' *stasima*, e.g. (*Hel.*) C. Wolff, *HSCP* 77 (1973), 61–84; (*Pho.*) M. B. Arthur, *HSCP* 81 (1977), 163–85.

15. See esp. Kranz (previous n.), pp. 235–41; Webster (1967), pp. 17–20; Rode in *Bauformen*, pp. 111–13; O. Panagl, *Die dithyrambischen Stasima des E.* (diss. Wien, 1967) and (*oratio recta* in them) *WS* 6 (1972), 5–18.

16. Lyric exchanges (and *stasima* and monody) in their dramatic and musical-poetic quality are best appreciated for English readers by Webster (1967), pp. 17–20, 282–7 and, more on formal aspects, his *The Greek Chorus* (London, 1970), pp. 143–9, 156–73, 209–11; cf. Barlow, pp. 56–60. H. Popp, 'Das Amoibaion', in *Bauformen*, pp. 221–75 is strong on form and metre, weak on other questions (and notes the little special literature).

17. W. Barner, 'Die Monodie', in *Bauformen*, pp. 277–320 is wide-ranging (278 n. 9 for the

thin literature to 1970, esp. Schadewaldt, pp. 14–19, 143–78). Barlow, pp. 43–60 illuminates monody's 'personal and subjective landscapes'.

Lyric metre: formal analysis is very difficult and disputed. O. Schröder, *Euripidis Cantica* (Leipzig, 1928²) needs replacement. Some songs in D. S. Raven, *Greek Metre* (London, 1962); A. M. Dale, *Metrical Analyses of Tragic Choruses I: Dactylo-Epitrite, BICS* Suppl. 21 (1971), 42–101 (more promised). Dale, *Coll. Papers*, pp. 257 f. ('Expressive Rhythm in Greek Drama', pp. 248–58, cf. 156–69) says most lyric is not susceptible to analysis at all in terms of emotional quality or ethos, but U. von Wilamowitz, *Griechische Verskunst* (Berlin, 1921) and her own *The Lyric Metres of Greek Drama* (Cambridge, 1968²) show what a sensitive ear can achieve. Also: J. Denniston in *Greek Poetry and Life* (G. Murray *Festschrift*) (Oxford, 1936), pp. 121–44 (iambics); N. C. Conomis, *Hermes* 92 (1964), 23–50 (dochmiacs); T. C. W. Stinton, *CQ* 27 (1977), 27–66 (pause and period); S. G. Brown, 'Metrical Innovations in E.'s Later Plays', *AJP* 95 (1974), 207–34. M. de Oliveria Pulquerio, *Caracteristicas metricas das monodias de E.* (Coimbra, 1969). A sequel to W. Kraus, *Strophengestaltung in der griechischen Tragödie I: Aischylos und Sophokles* (Wien, 1957) would be invaluable; it gives some help for E.

18. E.g.: naturalness, Ar. *Rhet.* 1404b24 f.; Long. *de subl.* 40.3 (see D. A. Russell's *Commentary*); fluency: Dion. Hal. *de comp. verb.* 23; simplicity: Hor. *A.P.* 95 f.; E.'s language like the comedian Philemon's: Satyrus, *vit. Eur.* POxy 1176.39. vii. 15–36. Cf. on *rhesis*, § (a) above.

19. Esp. Quint. *Inst. Or.* X.1.67–8 (depiction of feelings); Dio Chrys. XVIII.7; LII.11 (model for the man of affairs); cf. S. F Bonner, *Education in Ancient Rome* (London, 1977), esp. pp. 214–15. The ancient scholia at e.g. *Alc.* 779, *Tro.* 634, *Pho.* 388 criticize 'inappropriate philosophizing'; other references at Schmid, pp. 769 f.

20. T. Miller, *E. rhetoricus* (diss. Göttingen, 1887); J. T. Lees, *Dikanikos logos in E.* (Lincoln (U.S.A.), 1891); cf. Schmid, pp. 751–3. Perspective restored by F. Tietze, *Die eur. Reden und ihre Bedeutung* (Breslau, 1933), a dissertation of wide effect; now, e.g., R. L. Murray, *Persuasion in E.* (diss. Cornell, 1964). H. Friis Johansen, *General Reflection in Tragic Rhesis* (Copenhagen, 1959) (bibl.), is a model study of one feature, because it frequently illuminates the whole and not the particular context. Schadewaldt, as always, gives both detail and sensitive conspectus. For the *agon* in particular see n. 4 above.

21. Most treatments of *stichomythia* analyse its linguistic devices: see n. 9 above.

22. *Frogs* 1309 ff. (choral); 1331 ff., *Wasps* 317 ff., *Thes.* 1022 ff. (monodic); cf. § I n. 2 above.

23. Compendious exemplification, and older bibl., Schmid, pp. 790–812, esp. Kranz (n. 14 above); W. Breitenbach, *Untersuchungen zur Sprache der eur. Lyrik* (Stuttgart, 1934) (*Index Locorum* by K. H. Lee, Amsterdam, 1979); Smereka. More recently: E. Heitsch, *Zur lyrischen Sprache des E.* (diss Göttingen, 1955) (the 'intellectualism' of E.'s later lyric language); L. Bergson, *L'épithète ornamentale dans Eschyle, Sophocle et E.* (Uppsala, 1956). Bibl.: Lesky (1972), pp. 155 n. 1, 510 n. 12.

24. P. T. Stevens, *Colloquial Expressions in E.* (Wiesbaden, 1977) (bibl.), esp. pp. 64–8.

25. V. Pöschl, H. Gärtner, W. Heyke, *Bibliographie zur antiken Bildersprache* (Heidelberg, 1964). Specifically: K. Pauer, *Die Bildersprache des E.* (diss. Breslau, 1934); G. Rudberg, 'E.'s Naturgefühl', *SO* 12 (1933), 39–51; E. E. Pot, *De maritieme Beeldspraak bij E.* (diss. Utrecht, 1943); R. F. Stampfli, *The dramatic function of animals and animal imagery in … E.* (diss. Vanderbilt, 1971). Barlow, *Imagery* is the widest comparative study of intention, means, and effect.

26. *Hipp.*: respectively, C. P. Segal, *HSCP* 70 (1965), 117–69 and J. M. Bremer, *Mnem* 28 (1975), 268–80; *Bacc.*: W. S. Scott, *TAPA* 105 (1975), 333–46. For *Bacc.* also e.g. Conacher, pp. 73–7; *Med.* (the elements, animals) H. Musurillo, *AJP* 87 (1966), 52–74.

27. On such usage see Barlow, pp. 106 ff.; W. G. Arnott, *Mus.Phil.Lond.* 3 (1978), 14–20; in general e.g. Lattimore (1964), pp. 57 f.

28. These two songs wonderfully appreciated by T. C. W. Stinton, *E. and the Judgement of Paris* (London, 1965), pp. 13–25.

Additional Notes. General assessments of E.'s *poetry* are rare, e.g. Lattimore (1958), pp. 111 ff. For lexicography see my Appendix (vii).

V. IDEAS AND MEANINGS

The 'literary contest' in Aristophanes' *Frogs* has Euripides say that poets should be admired if they show cleverness and give good advice, and make their fellow citizens better men (1008–10). The purpose of that headline to the comic contest is clear, for it concentrates on Euripides' characters, and his intellectualism, as 'moral' influences on his audience;[1] but we might have expected his contemporaries, like ourselves, to want tragic poets rather to illuminate universals from divine and heroic myth. The plays in fact seldom give *direct* 'advice', and only by emphasizing the moral of the stage-action with general imperatives, e.g. *And.* 622–3 'suitors, make sure you marry daughters of good mothers!', 950, *Supp.* 917. Instead, Tragedy 'taught' by implication. Euripides' meanings are very hard to see, because of the rich diversity and inconsistency of his work.[2] He is constantly tensed between subscription to the mythic externals like story and ambience, and desire to create setting and persons immediate to the Athenians' ready experience; he is so clearly uncomfortable with the traditional religious and moral values which tragic myth enshrined; so variable from play to play in dramatic conception and individual ideas; so obviously 'modern' in the intellectual experimentation of his poetic style.

Later antiquity dubbed him the 'philosopher of the stage'; his contemporaries saw in him the suspect cleverness of the sophist (e.g. Ar. *Frogs* 771–6, *Lys.* 368). Greek *sophos* takes its meaning from context; it may connote knowledge, cleverness, or wisdom, and the skill to communicate them; Euripides often extolled it, like the virtue of clarity, *saphes* (*Or.* 397 equates them, in daring assonance: untranslatable!).[3] The qualities are indeed striking in Euripides: his lucidity of dialogue contrasts with later lyric overcleverness (see § IV (a) and (b) above); his dexterity of mind and restlessness of spirit may be explained largely from the intellectual ferment of his Athens.[4] Ancient sources assert his acquaintance with leading sophists or with Socrates – or at least with their ideas. Similarities and echoes are everywhere, sometimes apparent controversial engagement, but never consistently enough to justify the earlier modern view of Euripides as a publicist, in the guise of dramatist, for new theories or codes, let alone any one thinker's theories, a 'poet of the Enlightenment'.[5] The temptation to that view – and the necessary caution – may be seen in a few exemplary passages which attract most discussion.

Euripides sometimes appeals to an impersonal or abstract supreme power, like 'air' or 'ether' (*Hel.* 1015–16, fr. 919, 908b Snell; cf. the mockery of Ar. *Frogs* 892 'ether, my food of life'); or 'mind' (fr. 913.3 Snell, 1018, cf. *Tro*. 887 below). In a controlling 'mind' he echoes Anaxagoras, with 'ether' approaches Diogenes of Apollonia, who equated 'ether' with 'Zeus' – as Euripides himself does (fr. 877, 941.1–3, cf. 839.1–2). These fragments cannot, unfortunately, be located in plays or time, but Euripides varies so much anyway in his attribution of supreme power, or godhead, or its approximation to the traditional Olympians, that we may conclude only his continuous speculation about it – and a modernity or cynicism startling to Tragedy's ethos (e.g. fr. 286, the gods' apparent neglect of 'justice'). 'Whoever Zeus is', his persons say (*HF* 1263, *Tro*. 885, fr. 480), or 'whatever god is' (*Bacc*. 894, *Or*. 418, esp. *Hel*. 1137–8 'whatever is god, or not god, or the between'!). True, such words depend in part on a precautionary formula of prayer, very wide at *Tro*. 885–7 'whoever you are, Zeus, hard to place and know, whether natural necessity or mind of men . . .'; and the *Hel*. passage reflects a fashionable style of polar expression (see below) – but the inconsistencies are clear when they are set against the earlier quotations, and occasional doubt whether 'Zeus' or 'chance' governs the world, e.g. *Hec*. 488–91, or the gods or chance, e.g. fr. 154.4–5 Austin 'if chance is real, there's no need for gods; but if the gods have power, chance is nothing', cf. *El*. 490–1, *Ion* 1512; or against the agnosticism, or worse, of e.g. *Hel*. 711 'what an inconstant, indeterminable thing is god!'[6]

Some similar problems. When Medea acknowledges that 'my heart's anger is stronger than my deliberation' (*Med*. 1079), and Phaedra that 'I understand and know what is right, but do not carry it through' (*Hipp*. 380–1), these words crystallize conflicts which rule whole plays – but is Euripides also openly disputing the Socratic theory 'no one does wrong willingly'? In a continuing debate, some scholars think the reference in plays so close in time must indicate that; others that Euripides simply interested himself in a lively contemporary argument, which Socrates took up, the relation between virtue and knowledge.[7] Equally contentious were the questions whether human nature itself, inborn (Greek *phusis*), or education, determined ability;[8] and how natural behaviour related to social convention or law (Greek *nomos* covers both), and which of those three, or 'god', should guide man. Euripides writes with extreme ambiguity at e.g. *Hec*. 799–801 'we are but slaves, and weak with it; but the gods have power, together with their master, *nomos* ('law'?): for we worship the gods out of *nomos* ('convention'?), and live within the bounds of right and wrong'; contrast fr. 920 = 265a Snell 'nature wished it, which has no concern for law'.[9]

These passages and topics illustrate too the error of taking ideas uncritically from dramatic context, and collating them; episodic and especially rhetorical pressures vary too much, within and between plays.[10] Comparative assessment is made still harder by a prominent habit of thought and expression which Euripides owed also to sophistic influence: the antithetical mode. Apparently instinctive to the Greeks, and embryonic in Homer, the sophists developed it into an instrument of formal argumentation both conceptual and rhetorical. *Antiope* fr. XXI ed. Kambitsis (= fr. 189 Nauck) is often cited as emblematic: 'a man may make two sides to an argument on any matter, if he has a skill in speaking'. Polar statements and discussions, polar conceptions of setting and action, pervade Euripides: they govern single sentences or 'paragraphs', particularly the often sententious starts and ends of *rhesis*; they inform whole scenes, notoriously the *agon* – and even whole plays which depend on conflict and contrast, of whatever stamp or date (cf. § II(a) above). *Med.*, *Hipp.*, and *Bacc.* are the clearest examples, but also e.g. *Hel.*, with its ironic interplay of appearance and reality.[11]

So Euripides frequently expatiates or 'philosophizes' as context suggests a way of making its dramatic point immediate to the audience through familiar techniques of expression and argument, and by reference to its contemporary application. Two emphases individual to him show this style very well, his portrayal of women and his numerous 'political allusions'.

Early plays rely much on women's sins and sufferings, but women are prominent at any time, for their pathos or enterprise, or both (§ II(a) and (b) above); there is no doubt that they fascinated Euripides. Nearly all the plays comment in passing on their behaviour or status. Was Euripides condemning them, a misogynist as the comic poets would have him (e.g. Ar. *Lys.* 283, 368 f.; *Thes.* 383 ff., 453 ff.) – for example for their cunning, *Med.* 408–9, *Hec.* 884–5, *Hel.* 1621? or, in recognizing their social subjection (esp. *Med.* 231–51), was he contesting common prejudice against their talent and virtue, e.g. *Med.* 1086, *Supp.* 294, *Bacc.* 314–18? 'Good women are lost sight of for bad', state *Ion* 398–400, cf. fr. 493, 494, 657; these are self-defences in the plays, but the noble self-sacrificing wife or daughter is a favoured character, from *Alcestis* on (§§ II(b) and III(b) above).[12]

So lively was Euripides' interest in the totality of Athens' life, that he brought his *polis* into the mythic world more obviously and consistently than Sophocles and even Aeschylus. 'Anachronism' is a simple misnomer for this contemporaneity characteristic of all Tragedy (does it worry *us* in Shakespeare's Roman plays?). The special problem in Euripides is to measure the productive tensions thus created, as present microcosm and timeless macrocosm illuminate each other. Plays too, like all works of art, are documents of their age.[13] For some readers, political 'references' suggest programmatic interpretations – as if *Hcld.*

and *Supp.* were exclusively patrio-political texts, addressed to a narrow time. Others rightly see 'allusions', in plays of any date, as echoes of loud, contemporary predicament, which Euripides' responsive and open talent brought in for even greater immediacy.[14]

The clearest guide to Euripides' purpose will be a sense of each play's general meaning, where that can be taken; there are some plays whose parts are not easily reconciled, where dramaturgy is episodic (cf. §§ II(a) and III(a) above). Now Euripides is a dramatist of myth, and his general meaning will be his interpretation of it for his own day. In no aspect of his work does Euripides himself ask so many questions, leaving most unanswered, or scholarship seem able to reply only in kind. Did he ever allow myth to 'speak for itself'? Most directly in *Tro.*, perhaps, in the agony of war's victims, and the ominous if unrealized intention of the gods against the victors (*Tro.* 48–97). However 'modern' the psychology of Pentheus in *Bacc.*, however skilful the play's ambivalence, its power is elemental. But *HF* shows well the tension between poet and myth: the great hero's rescue of his family is late but happily seems to vindicate his divine parentage; then comes his sudden, inexplicable destruction; last, Euripides brings the mythic agony into his own time when Theseus persuades the hero of his duty to live on – but also promises his everlasting cult at Athens (1328–33). In *Hipp.* divine prologue and epilogue foretell and explain an action whose causality in the main persons is realistically and uncomfortably human; yet Hippolytus is destroyed physically by the coincidence of his father's banishment and Poseidon's bull.

What do such gods 'mean'? Everyone might agree that *Bacc.* contrasts transcending, 'religious' experience with a too human, frightened, and disastrous attempt to deny it – but does the play recognize or condemn a 'god', *the* god, Dionysus, or use him as a convenient symbol? Aphrodite and Artemis in *Hipp.*, too, for sex and its sublimation? Are Iris and Madness in *HF* – and these other gods – poetic instruments of man's terrifying vulnerability? Euripides arguably stresses such danger from inherent weakness, from defective understanding, from irrationality, from unforeseeable accident. Or are these plays superlative tragedy, in the universal sense, because they subordinate all human or circumstantial factors to a higher provision, a kind of justice, natural or absolute, or one superintended by the traditional Olympians? These plays present extreme problems of interpretation; it is part of their greatness.[15]

In many more plays the gods' overt role is small or non-existent (e.g. *Med.*, *Hec.*, *Supp.*, *IT*, *Hel.*, *Pho.*, *IA*); or the persons are only a little conscious of divine influence or need (e.g. *Alc.*, *And.*, *El.*, *Ion*).[16] It is said, Euripides here uses myth to illustrate man's greater freedom to determine and act for himself, for better or worse. If so, the limits of that freedom are made clear. There is the fact of life itself, and its obligations; and constraints of convention, social or moral; and the human uncertainties just mentioned. Euripides tests and retests them against the mythic paradigm of situation, action, and outcome. Human effort is either thwarted or promoted by accident, and even the happiest success often merely fulfils 'history' revealed by the *deus*.[17] Euripides seems torn between the ironic portrayal of man's ultimate helplessness, against himself or externals, both frequently irrational, and wishful assertion of man's independence. So it is possible to argue from the plays, now that he 'believed' and used myth as the vehicle of unchanging reality, now that he used it, perforce but inventively, to question every 'truth' about man and god it offered. Anyone attempting to write a 'philosophy of Euripides' must begin by admitting that he found no abiding faith in either.

NOTES

1. See K. J. Dover, *Aristophanic Comedy* (London, 1972), pp. 183–9; cf. Jones, pp. 239–42, Taplin (1977), pp. 166 f.

2. Lesky (1972), p. 520 cites a *bon mot* of H. D. F. Kitto, 'You never know where you are'. Interpretations of E., many despairing of synthesis, are reviewed by e.g. A. Rivier, *Essai sur le tragique d'E.* (Lausanne, 1944[1]), pp. 9–21 (Paris, 1975[2], pp. 3–27); A. Lesky, *AAHG* 2 (1949), 34–9; Greenwood pp. 1–91; J. C. Kamerbeek in *Entretiens*, pp. 3–6; Jones, pp. 268 f.; Conacher, pp. 12–14; H. Rohdich, *Die eur. Tragödie* (Heidelberg, 1968), pp. 13–16; Vellacott, pp. 2–8. The 'rationalist' view of A. W. Verrall was perpetuated by G. Norwood, *Essays on Euripidean Drama* (Cambridge, 1954), pp. 1–51; in the same vein Greenwood and Vellacott.

3. Schmid, pp. 318 n. 5, 690–1 nn. for the ancient references.

4. The classic modern statement is K. Reinhardt, 'Die Sinneskrise bei E.', in *Tradition und Geist* (Göttingen, 1960), pp. 223–56. Cf. esp. Lucas, pp. 175–6, 232–43; Webster (1967), pp. 21–9, Lesky (1967), pp. 133–7 and (1972), pp. 512–18 (bibl.). R. P. Winnington-Ingram, 'Euripides: Poietes Sophos', *Arethusa* 2 (1969), 127–42 is important.

5. W. Nestle, *E.: der Dichter der griechischen Aufklärung* (Stuttgart, 1901) was very influential (and remains the fullest collection of material); bibl. in Schmid, pp. 315–17, who p. 686 n. 1 notes that P. Masqueray, *E. et ses idées* (Paris, 1908) more accurately read E. as a mirror of contemporary thought.

6. The rôle of 'chance' in E.'s plays is much disputed. References and older bibl. in Schmid, p. 702 n. 4; played down by e.g. Webster (1967), p. 287 n. 16; allowed by e.g. Lesky (1972), pp. 424–5 (bibl.), cf. Lucas, p. 24, A. P. Burnett, *CPh* 55 (1960), 151–63 (on *Hel.*). Cf. § II n. 12 above, and n. 15 below.

7. Socratic controversy argued most strongly by Snell (1964), pp. 48–69, with fuller bibl. in (1971), p. 63 n. 62; cf. e.g. E. R. Dodds, *The Greeks and the Irrational* (Berkeley, 1951), pp. 186 f. (an earlier discussion of moral failing in *Hipp.* in *CR* 39 (1925), 102–4). Reserve by e.g. Barrett, ed. *Hippolytos* ad loc.; Conacher, p. 54; J. Moline, *Hermes* 103 (1975), 45–67. Thoughts like *Hipp.* 380–1 are found in fr. 840, 841, from the *Chrysippus*, also about irresistible (but pederastic) love, but the play cannot be dated; cf. fr. 572.4–5, from the late *Oenomaus*. For the difficult passage *Med.* 1021–80, esp. 1079, see H. Diller, *Hermes* 94 (1966), 267–75 and (bibl.) Lesky (1972), pp. 311–12; cf. § II n. 21 above.

8. Thematic importance for this question (*Hipp.* 79–80, *Supp.* 913–17, *Hec.* 599) was suggested by Lesky (1972), p. 514 n. 8.

IDEAS AND MEANINGS 35

9. F. Heinimann, *Nomos und Physis* (Basel, 1945) analyses the sophistic debate; cf. Dodds (n. 7 above), pp. 182 f. and e.g. Adkins (n. 14 below), pp. 106–12. For E. see Schmid, p. 725, Lucas, pp. 234–5, Lesky (1967), 172–3, Webster (1967), pp. 23–4. Also: J. de Romilly, *La loi dans la pensée grecque* (Paris, 1971).

10. Necessary warnings by e.g. Lucas, p. 242; Grube, pp. 80–98, esp. 92 ff.; Webster (1967), p. 290; Lesky (1967), p. 175 and (1972), p. 514; cf. § II n. 24 above.

11. On this quality of *Hel.* see G. Zuntz in *Entretiens*, pp. 199–241; Conacher, p. 290 n. 7 (bibl.); R. Kannicht's *Commentary* (Heidelberg, 1969); C. Segal, *TAPA* 102 (1971), 553–614. Myth and reality: J. Kamerbeek in *Entretiens*, pp. 1–41. Also: C. E. Luschnigg, *The logos-ergon conflict; a study of Euripidean tragedy* (diss. Cincinnati, 1972).

12. Women in E.: Schmid, pp. 321 f., 690 n. 6, 693 f. (references and bibl.); Lucas, pp. 242 f. (women hard to one another); Lesky (1967), pp. 140 f.; Vellacott, pp. 82–126 finds their 'precarious condition' a major theme. Women driven to wrong by men: J. C. Alsina, *Helmantica* 9 (1958), 87–131; to revenge by men's unfeeling designs (*Med.*), A. Dihle, *A & A* 22 (1976), 175–84.

13. So Murray's title; cf. Dodds, ed. *Bacchae*, Preface. Zuntz (1963), pp. 78–81; Walcot, pp. 76–103 (social values and background). Vellacott, pp. 17–19, 153–77 makes the tension a premiss of his interpretation. Cf. next n.

14. G. Zuntz, *Opusc. Selecta* (Manchester, 1972), pp. 54–61 (written 1954) corrected the excesses associated esp. with H. Grégoire, the 'Budé' editor, E. Delebecque, *E. et la guerre du Péloponnèse* (Paris, 1951), and R. Goossens, *E. et Athènes* (Bruxelles, 1962) (written 1945); these books nevertheless have referential value, like the similarly tinged V. di Benedetto, *E.: teatro e società* (Torino, 1971). Zuntz himself (1963) interprets the tension best, for *Hcld.* and *Supp.*; cf. Grube, pp. 29–36; Lucas, pp. 238–42; Lesky e.g. (1967), p. 159. Recently on e.g. *Or.*: J. de Romilly, *Studi ... Cataudella I* (Catania, 1972), pp. 237–51 (public condemnation to death) and W. Burkert, *A & A* 20 (1974), 97–109 (aristocratic resort to violence).

The plays are inevitably read as evidence for moral and political values. This risks making sociologist out of thinking poet who necessarily described dilemma and behaviour in contemporary terms, and ignoring other dangers of misinterpretation (n. 10 above). A. W. H. Adkins, *Moral Values and Political Behaviour in Ancient Greece* (London, 1972) (ref. to his earlier books) and *CQ* 16 (1966), 193–219 (*Hec.*, *HF*) does not wholly avoid it; L. Bergson, *Die Relativität der Werte im Frühwerk des E.* (Stockholm, 1971) is judiciously reviewed by O. Taplin, *CR* 24 (1974), 127–8.

Another extreme is to read the plays against a socio-political *credamus*. This approach, strongest in E. Europe, can seem coldly determined, but may rest on useful observation of detail and theme. H. Kuch, *Philologus* 123 (1979), 202–15 sets out the premisses, with copious bibl.; his own *Kriegsgefangenschaft und Sklaverei bei E.* (Berlin, 1974) (*And.*, *Hec.*, *Tro.*) leaves the work of art largely intact.

15. *HF* indeed causes despair: the play itself says, inescapably, that the madness is caused by the gods – as Heracles accepts (1303–8, cf. 1392–3), only to deny their credibility in poetic myth (1340–6); for this intractable problem see Lesky (1972), pp. 379–81 (bibl.); T. C. W. Stinton, *PCPS* 22 (1976), 82–4; A. L. Brown, *ib.* 24 (1978), 22–30. For *Hipp.* see e.g. R. G. Winnington-Ingram in *Entretiens*, pp. 169–97 (the gods symbolize the reality human nature and failing cannot escape); A. Köhnken, *Hermes* 100 (1972), 179–90 (divine prologue and epilogue stamp Hippolytus' illusion as truly tragic). For *Bacc.*, the most discussed of all plays (see *APh*!), see esp. R. P. Winnington-Ingram, *E. and Dionysus* (Cambridge, 1948) and E. R. Dodds' incomparable *Commentary* (Oxford, 1960²); (bibl.) Lesky (1972), pp. 484–99.

On gods and myth in E. Grube, pp. 41–62 writes very fairly; cf. e.g. Lucas, pp. 233–4 (E. a sceptic but accepting the poetry of myth); Conacher, esp. pp. 3–23 (grades of scepticism, satire, and disbelief corresponding to the prominence of action humanly motivated and determined); Lloyd-Jones, pp. 145–55 (protest against 'symbolic' interpretations); Vickers, pp. 279–337 and *passim* (myth used for its social and ethical implications, permitting E. richly diverse and profound criticism of man's failings). In general: Webster (1967), pp. 290–6; Matthiessen, pp. 173–86 (late plays); Lesky (1967: use Index) and (1972), pp. 514–22 (best bibl.).

16. Interesting that in these four plays the god is Apollo, who bears E.'s strongest criticism, especially for his oracular voice (a general condemnation, or of contemporary Delphic influence?), e.g. *And.* 1027–36, 1161–5; *El.* 979–81, 1245–6, 1302 – but contrast e.g. *El.* 399–400, 1247, *Ion*

IDEAS AND MEANINGS

1609–12, *Or.* 1666–7, *Pho.* 954–9. On e.g. *Ion* see Conacher, pp. 276–81, Lesky (1972), pp. 435–6.

17. A benevolent view of myth in *IT*, *Hel.*, and *Ion* is taken by C. H. Whitman, *E. and the Full Circle of Myth* (Harvard, 1974) ('plays of purity and redemption'). On the *deus* see esp. § II n. 13.

BIBLIOGRAPHICAL APPENDIX

(i) *Abbreviated References* (put here for convenience and economy; many important works are noted only in the relevant Section).

BARLOW, S. A., *The Imagery of Euripides* (London, 1971): unique in its range.

'Bauformen' = *Die Bauformen der griechischen Tragödie*, ed. W. Jens (München, 1971): on formal structures, well-documented but mostly too 'cold'.

CONACHER, D. J., *Euripidean Drama: Myth, Theme and Structure* (Toronto, 1967): best appreciation of its kind; good bibl. – but no index.

DALE, A. M., *Collected Papers* (Cambridge, 1969).

'Entretiens' = *Euripide, Entretiens sur l'Antiquité Classique VI* (Vandoeuvres-Genève, 1960): seven important papers and discussions.

FRIEDRICH, W. H., *Euripides und Diphilos* (München, 1953): dramatic and formal appreciations (*Ion, Hec., And., Tro., El., IA, Hipp.*).

GREENWOOD, L. H. G., *Aspects of Euripidean Tragedy* (Cambridge, 1953) (esp. *Hipp., Bacc., HF, Supp.*): interprets the plays as 'fictitious fantasies'.

GRUBE, G. M., *The Drama of Euripides* (London, 1961²): a 'handbook'.

JONES, J., *On Aristotle and Greek Tragedy* (London, 1962).

KITTO, H. D. F., *Greek Tragedy: a Literary Study* (London, 1961³): formal and stylistic critique.

LATTIMORE, R. (1958) = *The Poetry of Greek Tragedy* (Oxford, 1958) (esp. *Med., Hel., Bacc.*).

— (1964) = *Story Patterns in Greek Tragedy* (London, 1964).

LESKY, A. (1967) = *Greek Tragedy* (trans. H. A. Frankfort) (London, 1967²): sane, concerned basic text-book; excellent bibl.

— (1972) = *Die tragische Dichtung der Hellenen* (Göttingen, 1972³): exhaustive, richly documented, analytic – but poor index.

LLOYD-JONES, H., *The Justice of Zeus* (Berkeley, 1971).

LUCAS, D. W., *The Greek Tragic Poets* (London, 1959²): sound introduction.

LUDWIG, W., *Sapheneia* (Tübingen, 1954): clarity of structural expression in late Euripides; influential.

MATTHIESSEN, K., *Elektra, Taurische Iphigenie und Helena* (Göttingen, 1964): dramatic form and comparative chronology of late plays.

MURRAY, G., *Euripides and His Age* (London, (1913¹) 1946²): brilliant, ageless sketch.

RAU, P., *Paratragodia* (München, 1967): particularly illuminating for Euripides.

SCHADEWALDT, W., *Monolog und Selbstgespräch* (Berlin, 1926): wide-ranging, influential.

SCHMID, W., *Geschichte der griechischen Literatur*, I.3 (München, 1940).

SMEREKA, L., *Studia Euripidea*, I and II.1 (Lwow, 1936–7): minute lexical study.

SNELL, B. (1964) = *Scenes from Greek Drama* (Berkeley, 1964).

— (1971) = *Szenen aus griechischen Dramen* (Berlin, 1971).

STEIDLE, W., *Studien zum antiken Drama* (München, 1968): interaction of the visual and the dramatic (*Bacc., Hec., Tro., El., Or., And., Alc., Med.* emphasized).

STROHM, H., *Euripides: Interpretationen zur dramatischen Form* (München, 1957).

TAPLIN, O. (1977) = *The Stagecraft of Aeschylus* (Oxford, 1977): very important for all Tragedy.

— (1978) = *Greek Tragedy in Action* (London, 1978): best short study of its kind, visualizing performance (*Hipp., Ion, Bacc.* emphasized).

VELLACOTT, P., *Ironic Drama: a Study of Euripides' Method and Meaning* (Cambridge, 1976): the plays hide radical criticism of society.

VICKERS, B., *Towards Greek Tragedy* (London, 1973).
WALCOT, P., *Greek Drama in its Theatrical and Social Context* (Cardiff, 1976).
WEBSTER, T. B. L. (1967) = *The Tragedies of Euripides* (London, 1967): emphasizes lost plays; attempts many suggestive generalizations; undervalued.
— (1968) = 'Greek Tragedy', in *Fifty Years (and Twelve) of Classical Scholarship* (Oxford, 1968), pp. 88–122.
ZUNTZ, G. (1963) = *The Political Plays of Euripides* (Manchester, 1963²): *Supp.* and *Hcld.* 'rehabilitated'; seminal work.
— (1965) = *An Inquiry into the Transmission of the Plays of Euripides* (Cambridge, 1965): important detailed and historical sketch.

(ii) *Bibliography*: annual since 1924 in *APh*. *Evaluative* surveys: periodically in *AAHG* since 1948 (see esp. 1949, covering 1935–48, by A. Lesky; 1973, 1974, 1976, 1977 by H. Strohm); Webster (1968); H. W. Miller, *CW* 49 (1956), 81–92 (for 1940–54) and 60 (1967), 177–9, 182–7, 218–20 (1955–65); H. van Looy, *AC* 39 (1970), 528–62 (for 1967/70). Composite by plays and topics: Schmid, pp. 309–842, 858–71 (exhaustive till 1939); Lesky (1972), pp. 275–522, cf. 11–16, 155 n. 1, 156 n. 2, 159 n. 7, 162 n. 22, 262 n. 1 (emphasis on 20th C.); cf. K. Matthiessen, 'Euripides', in *Das griechische Drama*, ed. G. Seeck (Darmstadt, 1979), pp. 105–54. Fragments: H. van Looy, *AC* 32 (1963), 162–99, 607–8; Webster (1967) is very full.

(iii) *Editions*: (a) *Complete plays*: G. Murray's OCT (1902¹–1913³) is standard until replaced by J. Diggle's (Vol. II first, 1981: *Supp., El., HF, Tro., IT, Ion*). The *Bibliotheca Teubneriana* issues individual plays, with various editors (Leipzig, 1964–); uneven, but all volumes have select bibliographies. (b) *Fragments*: A. Nauck's *Tragicorum Graecorum Fragmenta* (Leipzig, 1889², repr. Hildesheim 1964 with *Supplementum* by B. Snell) is standard until replaced by Vol. V: *Euripides*, ed. R. Kannicht, of the new *TrGF*. For larger pieces found since Nauck see esp. D. L. Page, *Select Papyri III: Literary* ('Loeb') (London, 1942), pp. 54–135; C. Austin, *Nova Fragmenta Euripidea in Papyris Reperta* (Berlin, 1968); some fragmentary plays now have annotated editions. The fragments have been renumbered and documented but not re-edited by H. J. Mette, *Lustrum* 12–13 (1967–8), 5–288, 289–403; 17 (1973–4), 5–26; 19 (1976), 65–78.

(iv) *English Translations*: D. Grene, R. Lattimore (eds.), *The Complete Greek Tragedies* (Chicago, 1955–9) is accurate, sensitive, stylish. P. Vellacott ('Penguin Classics') (London, 1953–72) is readable, actable, not always reliable. Excellent prose versions of *Alc., Bacc., El., Ion, Med.* by D. W. Lucas (London, Cambridge, 1949–55). A planned, much needed replacement of A. S. Way's 'Loeb' (1912) was cancelled in 1976. Cf. (v) below, for *Alc., Bacc., IA, Ion*.

(v) *Commentaries* (English only): F. A. Paley, *Euripides* (3 vols.) (London, 1857¹–1889³), workmanlike and honest, is still useful. Among school-editions between 1880 and 1914 look esp. for those by Earle, Hadley, Harry, Headlam, Paley. In the 'Clarendon' *Euripides* individuals annotate Murray's OCT with varying emphases (8 vols., *Alc., And., Bacc., El., Hel., Ion, IT, Med.* (Oxford, 1938–71), more planned; *Composite Index* by C. Collard (Groningen, 1981)). J. Diggle, *Studies on the Text of Euripides* (Oxford, 1980) annotates Vol. II of his new OCT.

Also: *Alc.*: C. R. Beye (Englewood Cliffs, 1974) (trans. only, comm.). *And.*: K. M. Aldrich (Lincoln (U.S.A.), 1961) (no text, 'running' comm. with nn.; bibl.). *Bacc.*: R. P. Winnington-Ingram, *Euripides and Dionysus* (Cambridge, 1948) (no text, 'running' comm.); G. S. Kirk (Cambridge, 1979²) (trans. only, comm.). *Cyc.*: R. G. Ussher (Roma, 1978) (bibl.). *Hec.*: M. Tierney (Dublin, 1946, repr. Bristol, 1979) (schools). *Hel.*: A. C. Pearson (Cambridge, 1903). *Hcld.*: A. C. Pearson (Cambridge, 1907); cf. Zuntz (1963), pp. 26–54, 97–128. *Hipp.*: W. S. Barrett (Oxford, 1964). *Ion*: A. P. Burnett (Englewood Cliffs, 1970) (trans. only, comm.). *IA*: E. B. England (London, 1891); K. Cavander (Englewood Cliffs, 1970) (trans. only, comm.). *Med.*: A. F. Elliott (Oxford, 1969) (schools). *Or.*: N. Wedd (Cambridge, 1895). *Pho.*: A. C. Pearson (Cambridge, 1909); J. U. Powell (London, 1911). *Supp.*: C. Collard (Groningen, 1975) (2 vols.; bibl.). *Tro.*: K. H. Lee (London, 1976) (bibl.). Fragmentary plays: *Alexandros*: R. A. Coles, *BICS* Suppl. 32 (1974) (bibl.); *Hypsipyle*: G. W. Bond (Oxford, 1963, corr. repr. 1969) (bibl.); *Phaethon*: J. Diggle (Cambridge, 1970) (bibl.); *Telephus*: E. W. Handley, J. Rae, *BICS* Suppl. 5 (1957). (*Rhesus*: W. H. Porter (Cambridge, 1929²); cf. my § I n. 12 above).

For older and foreign comms. see Schmid, pp. 840–1, Lesky (1972), p. 286 and (both) on individual plays. Since Lesky: *Bacc.*: J. Roux (Lyons, 1970–2) (2 vols., bibl.); H. Oranje (Amsterdam, 1979) (diss., 'running' comm. sub-titled 'The Play and its Audience', bibl.); *Antiope*: J. Kambitsis (Athènes, 1972) (bibl.); *Cresphontes*: O. Musso (Milano, 1974) (bibl.); *Erechtheus*: A. M. Diez (Granada, 1976) (bibl.).

New commentaries are planned for *Cyc.* (R. Seaford), *Hec.* (K. Matthiessen, German), *Hcld.* (D. Bain), *HF* (G. W. Bond), *IA* (W. Ritchie), *Or.* (C. W. Willink), *Pho.* (J. Bremer, D. Mastronarde), *Tro.* (P. G. Mason) – and needed for *El.*, *Ion*, *IT*, *Med.* (but see J. Diggle, above).

(vi) *Scholia*: E. Schwartz (Berlin, 1887–91) (2 vols.); new, more widely based edition needed.

(vii) *Lexicography*: Smereka (bibl.); J. T. Allen, G. Italie, *A Concordance to E.* (Berkeley, 1953), with *Supplement* by C. Collard (Groningen, 1971), who plans a Lexicon (*BICS* 18 (1971), 134–42); further supplemented by H. J. Mette, *Lustrum* 17 (1973–4), 25–6 and 19 (1976), 74–8. M. McDonald has begun to issue for each play *A Semi-lemmatized Concordance to E.* (Irvine, 1977–).

(viii) '*Nachleben*': special section in *APh* since 1970. F. L. Lucas, *E. and his Influence* (New York, 1922); Schmid, pp. 819–38; H. Funke, *Jahrb.f.d.Alt.u.Chr.* 8–9 (1965–6), 233–79; U. Petersen, *Goethe und E.* (Heidelberg, 1974). Drama: Friedrich; K. von Fritz, *Antike und moderne Tragödie* (Berlin, 1962); T. B. L. Webster, *Introduction to Menander* (London, 1974), pp. 56–67; A. G. Katsouris, *Tragic Patterns in Menander* (Athens, 1975) (bibl., p. 2 n. 2); R. J. Tarrant, 'Senecan Drama and its Antecedents, *HSCP* 82 (1978), 213–63 (important antidote). Also: W. H. Friedrich, 'E. in der lat. Literatur', *Hermes* 69 (1934), 300–15; B. Fenik, *The Influence of E. on Vergil's Aeneid* (diss. Princeton, 1960).